Illustrat

Project management in real terms

Illustrating PRINCE2®

Project management in real terms

SUSAN TUTTLE

IT Governance Publishing

Every possible effort has been made to ensure that the information contained in this book is accurate at the time of going to press, and the publisher and the author cannot accept responsibility for any errors or omissions, however caused. Any opinions expressed in this book are those of the author, not the publisher. Websites identified are for reference only, not endorsement, and any website visits are always at the reader's own risk. No responsibility for loss or damage occasioned to any person acting, or refraining from action, as a result of the material in this publication can be accepted by the publisher or the author.

PRINCE2® is a registered trade mark of the Cabinet Office. The Swirl logo™ is a trade mark of the Cabinet Office.

© Crown copyright 2009. All rights reserved. Material in italic bold is reproduced with the permission of the Cabinet Office under delegated authority from the Controller of HMSO.

Apart from any fair dealing for the purposes of research or private study, or criticism or review, as permitted under the Copyright, Designs and Patents Act 1988, this publication may only be reproduced, stored or transmitted, in any form, or by any means, with the prior permission in writing of the publisher or, in the case of reprographic reproduction, in accordance with the terms of licences issued by the Copyright Licensing Agency. Enquiries concerning reproduction outside those terms should be sent to the publisher at the following address:

IT Governance Publishing
IT Governance Limited
Unit 3, Clive Court
Bartholomew's Walk
Cambridgeshire Business Park
Ely
Cambridgeshire
CB7 4EH
United Kingdom
www.itgovernance.co.uk

© Susan Tuttle 2012
The author has asserted the rights of the author under the Copyright, Designs and Patents Act, 1988, to be identified as the author of this work.

First published in the United Kingdom in 2012
by IT Governance Publishing.

ISBN 978-1-84928-325-0

PREFACE

Using and understanding PRINCE2® comes second nature to me. I am a born project manager and practitioner of the method in both my professional and private lives. That may sound strange, but that is how much I believe in this methodology. I see how it can be used and tailored to any project in any environment, at any time and with anyone – be it work-related or not.

On every training course I teach, I share my love of organized fun with my course delegates. By the end of each course, they too love it. They actually get it and leave wanting to apply it to their own lives (probably only their work lives, but that's still a start!). Now, I want to share this passion with you. My illustrations come from my own experience and from those people I've had the pleasure of working with and/or training. All names and places have been modified to protect the innocent, naïve or culpably disobedient.

ABOUT THE AUTHOR

Susan Tuttle has 20 years of experience in projects and program and change management. She has a proven track record of producing exceptional results across diverse industries. She started her career in the financial industry in the US, before moving to IT consulting and earning her masters in training and development.

After moving to the UK in 2004, Susan became an accredited trainer in PRINCE2®, MSP® and change management. Her training style is influenced by her strong commitment to human development, which is continually demonstrated in her use of learner-centered adult learning theories and principles. She is an energetic self-starter with excellent analytical, organizational, and creative skills.

ACKNOWLEDGEMENTS

Thank you to my mentor and friend, Melanie Franklin, for inspiring me to always do more. Thank you to my friends and family, especially my husband, Tony Leigh, for supporting me in my efforts to write this book.

We would like to acknowledge the following reviewers of this book for their useful contributions: Colin Bentley, ex-Chief Examiner PRINCE2®; Louise Blyth, Director, Blyth Softcom; Narinder Dhaliwal, Director, You Learn Limited; Darren Ley, Training Consultant, DLeytraining and Michelle Rowland, Director, You Learn Limited.

CONTENTS

INTRODUCTION

This book can be used as a guide to understanding the PRINCE2® framework. It uses everyday language and everyday experiences. By providing a real-life context around the method, the translations and illustrations will provide evidence of how to use (and how not to use) the PRINCE2® method.

Each topic in this book is broken into three subsections. The first subsection will provide a basic background for the PRINCE2® subject being investigated. The second will attempt to translate that subject into layman's terms. Finally, an illustration will give even more clarification and enable further insight into the given area of project management.

Example layout

PRINCE2® assertion

This section will provide a short summary or the basics of the method, as depicted in the PRINCE2® 2009 OGC guide. Each direct quote from the PRINCE2® guide will be represented in bold and italicized text to distinguish it from the author's text.

What this means

This section will attempt to highlight key points from the PRINCE2® method to aid an understanding of the meaning and context of the topic.

Note: For Chapter 15 ("Management Products"), the "What this means" section is replaced with one entitled, "When is it created? When is it updated?"

Illustration

This section offers a snippet, an example, or a story in real-world terms of people or companies using or misusing the PRINCE2® method.

Note: For Chapters 13 to 15 ("Tailoring PRINCE2®," "Roles" and "Management Products") a two-tiered illustration is provided, which shows how to tailor these aspects of PRINCE2® down for small projects and up for large ones.

For a full, more in-depth explanation of the method and the best-practice references, please see the official OGC product: *Managing Successful Projects with PRINCE2®*, OGC (2009).

CHAPTER 1: PRINCE2® OVERVIEW

Principles

Overview

Principles provide a framework of good practice for those people involved in a project. They are characterized as:

- *Universal in that they apply to every project*
- *Self-validating in that they have been proven in practice over many years*
- *Empowering because they give practitioners of the method added confidence and the ability to influence and shape how the project will be managed.*

What this means

According to *www.businessdictionary.com*, guiding principles can be defined as a "broad philosophy that guides an organization throughout its life in all circumstances, irrespective of changes in its goals, strategies, type of work, or the top management." Principles in the PRINCE2® approach can be defined similarly. Seven underlying principles should be applied to every project, regardless of what is going on inside or outside the project environment. They are sound, proven rules, which can be used as guideposts on the way to project success.

Illustration

By no means was Jermina's project perfect, yet she and her project management team received a company-sponsored award for excellence in project management. Jermina had followed the PRINCE2® principles throughout her project. She demonstrated the principles on a daily basis, which helped the project end on a successful note.

Decisions on her project did not have to come at a cost to the people and resources working on it. Instead, they were made objectively, with a concentration on confirming Continued Business Justification (Principle one). When new changes were required, no one took it personally. It either made business sense to include the change or to continue with the project without the change, depending on the impact on the business case. When things went horribly wrong, the Manage by Exception principle (Principle five) enabled the team to get the right information to the right level of management, who could make an expedient and appropriate decision for the project. It worked like clockwork.

Everyone on the team was encouraged to Learn from Experience (Principle two). With each issue, a lesson was captured and learned. Mistakes that were made were not repeated. On the other hand, positive lessons were always shared and frequently repeated. The team adhered to their defined roles and responsibilities, managed the project in stages, and tailored the method to suit their particular circumstances. The Focus on Products principle (Principle six) allowed all the team members to work creatively, so that they could contribute to and produce the best possible products – ones that were fit for purpose and supported the overall justification for the project.

For all their hard work and effort through all the ups and downs that come with managing a project, the team were recognized and rewarded by their company for sticking to the principles.

Themes

Overview

The PRINCE2® themes describe aspects of project management that must be addressed continually. Any project manager who gives thorough attention to these themes will fulfill the role in a professional manner.

All seven themes must be applied in a project but they should be tailored according to the scale, nature and complexity of the project concerned.

What this means

Rules are not meant to be broken. Nor are they meant to be rigid, harsh and unyielding, regardless of the circumstances. They are meant to be helpful in allowing groups of people to get from one point to another without having to rely on gut instincts, or worry about personality differences, politics and/or conflicts. Themes in PRINCE2® introduce the idea of seven areas of project management that should be considered in order to set the right level of rules (restrictions, constraints, limitations, controls, etc.), this depending on the project's unique set of circumstances.

Illustration

Ever play MONOPOLY according to the rules provided by Parker Brothers (the game publisher) without any deviations? Either due to time restrictions, boredom levels or attention spans (these dependent on the immediate situation or the type, age, or size of group playing), most people generate their own set of house rules for MONOPOLY. Some people put a time limit on the whole game and rule that whoever has the most money by the end of that time wins. Other players put limits on amounts to be borrowed from the bank, ensuring the faster demise of some of the players – and thus the overall game. Regardless of the reasons behind them, the house rules are there to suit the situation. They are agreed upfront and adhered to throughout the game. If they don't work for the players, they can be adjusted with a group consensus, and the new set of house rules will then be used to finish off the game.

Processes

Overview

PRINCE2® is a process-based approach for project management. A process is a structured set of activities designed to accomplish a specific objective. It takes one or more defined inputs and turns them into defined outputs.

What this means

Just as you don't bake a cake before you've mixed the ingredients, it is important to consider the separate activities involved in a project before starting it. The idea behind

PRINCE2® processes is to give a sense of the natural order to the activities of a project. Some will have to be modified and adjusted according to the individual project characteristics, but the seven processes help provide guidance on what should be done when, according to best practice.

Illustration

An organization reviewed a recently completed project to determine if it was worth the money they had invested in it. In order to conduct the review, the administration staff in the projects office were told to retroactively research the history of the project. They were to look specifically at what problem was being addressed, what options they had available at the time to deal with it – these including the option that was finally chosen – and identify which of the benefits, if any, that are now being seen in the organization can be tied back to this effort.

According to the information uncovered, the project had gone over budget and over time, and had only superficially addressed the original problem. Additionally, it had left the organization with higher-than-anticipated operating costs to maintain the new solution. An attempt was made to retrofit the benefits, but no solutions were found. A second version of the project was then commissioned to fix these new problems.

Wouldn't this assessment have been better placed at the beginning of the first project? A properly understood problem, approach and solution could have been identified and defined at the start of the project, instead of after, when it was too late. Somehow, there never seems to be enough time and/or money to start a project off well, but there's always enough to do it again!

CHAPTER 2: SEVEN PRINCIPLES

Principle one: Continued Business Justification

PRINCE2® assertion

A PRINCE2® project has continued business justification.

What this means

Not only should a project be justified in its original expenditure commitment, but the reasons behind it should remain valid throughout the entire expenditure. If the reasons disappear, a decision should be made by management to continue at a loss or stop the effort.

Illustration

A jilted bride, whose fiancé has recently dumped her for one of the bridesmaids, has a decision to make. She has already paid her deposit for the wedding hall. The reason for paying for the wedding was that there was going to be a wedding. The benefits of being a happy, loving couple starting out their lives together far outweighed the expense of hiring out the hall. Now that the wedding has been called off, does it make sense to continue to pay for it? It depends, of course.

If the bridegroom had dumped the bride one year or more before the wedding, the bride could have recouped her deposit without any penalty fees. If it had happened six months prior to the wedding, the bride may have lost the deposit, but could still cancel without having to pay the full price. However, what if the bridegroom's disappearing act occurred on the wedding day itself? All the costs would already have been spent, but none of the original benefits would actually be realized. Is it still worth having the reception party, even without the groom? Sounds like this matter might need to be escalated to corporate or program management (perhaps the father and/or mother of the bride? Or family attorneys?)

Principle two: Learn from Experience

PRINCE2® assertion

PRINCE2® project teams learn from previous experience: lessons are sought, recorded and acted upon throughout the life of the project.

What this means

This assertion centers on the idea that we should take time to review and reflect on past experiences to make future ones easier, faster and better. If we jump too fast into the doing of a project – without looking back at what has been done before – we will either be doomed to repeat our mistakes or be doomed to recreate the wheel every time we start something new.

Illustration

Six years ago, company X found themselves in a situation where their headquarters office was the only one that had access to and control of any of the company policies. Satellite offices around the country and around the world complained of not being able to tailor work to suit their local needs. A project was immediately put in place.

Three years later, the new chief executive officer (CEO) at the headquarters office inquired about the set of policies and procedures used at the organization in order to fully understand the work being done around the world. No one could provide a full set, as each satellite office had their own way of recording and documenting procedures. The new CEO immediately put in place a project to centralize all the records – including all the policies and procedures – in order to capitalize on a streamlined system of operating.

Today, at the annual board meeting, managers from the satellite offices complained of being oppressed and manipulated into using a set of stringent and inflexible procedures that were irrelevant to their specific local and regional needs. And the story continues.

Advice for company X would be to implement the Learn from Experience principle immediately. First of all, they would need to reflect on previous projects and the reasons behind them. Is the company stuck in a cycle of repetitive change for the sake of change? Sometimes, projects can be used to distract management away from more fundamental problems within the organization. If it is determined that this latest move to centralize (or decentralize) is truly required in the current circumstances facing the organization, then what went well and what went badly during the previous swings must be reflected on again. Use the previous experiences as a benchmark to improve against (in terms of project management competencies and maturity levels, at the very minimum).

Principle three: Defined Roles and Responsibilities

PRINCE2® assertion:

A PRINCE2® project has defined and agreed roles and responsibilities within an organization structure that engages the business, user and supplier stakeholder interests.

What this means

For every job, there is a portion (hopefully not a huge one) that is considered boring. Nobody likes doing the boring stuff. If we had our choice, we'd only do things that were fun. But if everyone only worked on the fun stuff, none of the boring stuff would ever get done. The Defined Roles and Responsibilities principle ties into the importance of assigning the right task to the right role and the right role to the right person/people. This way, everyone will be clear on what they are signing up to do, and have full knowledge of both the fun and the boring stuff.

Illustration

Everyone knows that a football (soccer) team has 11 players on a pitch at any one time. Each player is responsible for his/her position. If players started playing different positions willy-nilly, then there would be 11 strikers and no keeper. Everyone would be stepping all over each other trying to get the goal. With too many cooks in the kitchen, so to speak, there'd be no one playing defense, and the opposing team would have an easy time scoring.

Every player on the team needs to know where they should be playing and where the others should be, at all times. That isn't to say that a defensive player can't take advantage of a lucky breakaway and run the ball up the pitch towards the goal; if that were to happen, at least one of his teammates would stay behind to cover his position. Everyone would feel confident that the pitch was being properly manned at all times.

Principle four: Manage by Stages

PRINCE2® assertion:

A PRINCE2® project is planned, monitored and controlled on a stage-by-stage basis.

What this means

Can you predict the future? No one can with any guarantees. The best one can do is to take a best guess at what they think the future will be. But that is all it can be: a best guess. If one were to take a best guess about the details of the next five years, they would undoubtedly get it incredibly wrong. Even if they had every fact and figure from all that had happened in the past, they could never accurately predict details of the future. Instead, a better option would be to take a stab at prejudging the details of the near future and provide a broad, best-guess picture of the long-term future.

Illustration

Jenny knew she wanted to travel for a year after graduating from university. She would use the trip as a reward to herself for completing her degree. She used this goal as a focal point to get her through the doldrums of studying and revision sessions. However, with over two years to go, she could not, with any certainty, predict the exact details of what flight she would take, how many days after graduation she would leave, or any of the minute details about her trip. Instead, she broke her plans into manageable steps, which she dealt with one by one, in the buildup toward her sabbatical.

When she finally stepped on the plane for the first leg of her trip, she had all the right visas and all the right vaccinations. If she had planned these details at the beginning – three years ago – she would have had the wrong ones. Visa and vaccination requirements are constantly changing with the times and events of the world. Luckily, she planned the details for these only at the stage (the final one) where they were needed and could be predicted with accuracy.

Principle five: Manage by Exception

PRINCE2® assertion:

A PRINCE2® project has defined tolerances for each project objective to establish limits of delegated authority.

What this means

Senior managers take on a lot of responsibility when signing up to be project board members. However, they can't usually afford to dedicate more than a minimal amount of effort and time to complete the project. Rather, they rely quite heavily on the project manager to control the day-to-day management, while they continue to run their departments or directorates and continue to attend the innumerable meetings required of them. So how do they take ownership of something that they don't actually execute themselves? They delegate power down to the project manager in the form of change authority and tolerances. Change authority is the delegated responsibility for the consideration of changes, while tolerances are the permissible deviations from a plan's target(s).

As long as the project manager is working within their agreed authority levels, s/he is allowed to get on with the work. The project manager is required to provide periodic progress reports to prove s/he is operating with his/her limits. If a situation takes him/her outside of these limits, she/he must immediately escalate the situation – also known as an exception situation.

Illustration

When a new project manager is delegated a stage with zero tolerances and zero change authority, this might indicate that the project board either does not trust him/her, or does not have confidence in him/her. However, if after several successful stages the project board still will not relinquish any stage-level tolerance and/or change authority, then the project manager may infer one of two very likely scenarios. Either the project board members still do not trust him/her, or they are a tyrannical band of micromanagers. They will want to appear to be delegating responsibility for the project one stage at a time, but really they are ensuring that they are heavily involved in absolutely every decision that deviates from the stage plan. With even the tiniest of issues pulling the project manager outside his/her stage-level tolerance, or the tiniest of change requests being above his/her change authority, every issue or change becomes an exception – which requires an exception report and, thus, the project board's involvement.

On the other hand, when a project manager is being delegated an enormous amount of stage tolerance, it does not indicate that the project board has copious amounts of trust in him/her. It is more likely that the project board members understand the time pressures of their other commitments (running a department or sponsoring other change initiatives, for example) and recognize that they may not have a lot of time to give to this project. Thus, with high amounts of stage tolerance, the project manager is bound to be able to stay within their limits and, therefore, will not need to interrupt the project board with exceptions.

Principle six: Focus on Products

PRINCE2® assertion:

A PRINCE2® project focuses on the definition and delivery of products, in particular their quality requirements.

What this means

It is easy, and often natural, for people to start planning out a piece of work by focusing on what activities are required to get the work done. However, with a focus on the activities and the journey, it is easy to go off on a tangent away from the desired end goal: the finished products. Principle six asserts that attention must be given to the products every step of the way as, otherwise, it becomes easy to lose sight of what is important and get caught up in the politics, obstacles and unnecessary details of the end result.

Illustration

Allison really wanted a bicycle for her birthday. She mentioned it, dropped hints and gave obvious signs that this was what she desired. Eventually, her husband, Andrew, finally "heard" her and started the ball rolling.

He spent hours on the Internet researching road bikes, mountain bikes for off-road riding, and trick bikes for freestyle jumping and stunts. He decided on mountain bikes because of their superior safety features. He then spent his lunch hours, Saturday mornings and a few evenings looking at and testing mountain bikes. He invited Allison's friend,

Mary, to help him choose between the two he liked best. Mary was of a similar size and shape to Allison, so her input was essential. When, at last, he had decided on the type, size and color (Allison's favorite, of course), he ordered it. It was to be delivered on Allison's actual birthday, so it could be a surprise.

If only Allison had been clear about her expectations from the beginning, and not relied on clandestine clues. Getting a new bike was one of her birthday wishes, of course, but spending time with her husband was what she was really after. The bike was merely a means to an end. She had her heart set on the experience of the two of them perusing over new bikes, finding the one that spoke to both of them, and possibly even buying two, so they could ride together and spend even more time together. Instead, she got herself an absent husband who'd been spending more time with her close friend than he had with her, and a really heavy cardboard box on her doorstep (with no card!).

Principle seven: Tailor to Suit the Project Environment

PRINCE2® assertion:
PRINCE2® is tailored to suit the project's environment, size, complexity, importance, capability and risk.

What this means

A one-size-fits-all strategy rarely works for anything, much less large investments in project work, which are inherently unique and different from other work. Principle seven requires the project management team to consider the special characteristics of each project and tailor PRINCE2® – a best practice framework – to fit the needs of the project, rather than to force the project to fit PRINCE2®.

Illustration

A dressmaker, commissioned to make one bridal gown (size 12) and one dress for the maid of honor (size 16), is expected – if not required – to tailor the dresses to suit the separate measurements of the two women, rather than to create two size 14 dresses (the average size of the two women). Additionally, the gowns need to be of different fabrics, colors and complexities. The bride, wanting to wear a white, floor-length gown, should not be upstaged by her maid of honor, also wearing a white, floor-length gown.

CHAPTER 3: SEVEN THEMES

Theme one: Business Case

Purpose
The purpose of the Business Case theme is to establish mechanisms to judge whether the project is (and remains) desirable, viable and achievable as a means to support decision-making in its (continued) investment.

What this means

The business case sets out the case to the business. "Please give us (the project team) your money today, and we will create products that will result in benefits in the future" would be a business case, for example. It may seem that businesses must take a gamble on one project idea over all the others. But with solid research, diligent fact-finding, and careful financial assessment, the gamble can also be seen as taking a calculated risk.

Illustration

Over the last few years, politicians have been trying to persuade the general public that the solution to our pending electricity shortages is nuclear power. They show us pages and pages of facts and figures demonstrating the huge benefits of nuclear power (which include increased supplies, supply as and when we need it, and its ability to cope with growing demands – especially when oil runs out) mapped up against the costs – which are relatively low, even with maintenance and waste costs included. The one thing they don't tend to focus on – even though it's pretty much the only thing we, their constituents, can see – is the risk! One fault, one mistake, one accident and we, the constituents, may not be here anymore.

A good business case maps out all three aspects: the expected benefits, the costs (including ongoing sustainable costs) and the risks to give you the true story. It will also be updated periodically to prove that the continued expenditure against the effort is still worth it – what if a completely safe alternative energy source were discovered halfway through the project?

Theme two: Organization

Purpose:

The purpose of the Organization theme is to define and establish the project's structure of accountability and responsibilities (the 'who'?).

What this means

When lines of reporting are clearly drawn and people know whom they are to report to and who is to report to them, they can concentrate on how to get the work done. If these essential lines have not been clarified, then people will either be frightened into inaction – not knowing if they have authority to act – or end up stepping on each others' toes, each person thinking they have the authority over the other. Either way, conflict and chaos normally ensues.

Illustration

Bill and Annie belonged to the same gym. They regularly ran into each other there after work, and sometimes at the weekends. Back at work, Annie was a financial expert working as the team manager for a major project. Bill was the executive of that project. After work one night, Annie bumped into Bill at the gym and told him of a concern she had had earlier that day about some of the figures she was working on. She was going to call Bob, the project manager, the next day, but since she and Bill were both at the gym, she let him know about the problem there and then. When Bill went home that night, he started working remotely, investigating the problem, crunching numbers and sending e-mail after e-mail to try to find a solution. He worked long into the wee hours of the morning to no result.

The next morning, Bill showed Annie his work, and they reviewed the numbers again. Both Bill's and Annie's administration staff were helping out by pulling up old databases, perusing old spreadsheets, and dusting off old accounts. No one was getting any closer to the solution. Finally, some time around lunchtime, in a desperate call Annie phoned Bob, the project manager. She asked him if he had access to an old record on a latent database that she thought might have some clues. Confused by her request, he enquired about her reasons. Annoyed and frustrated, Annie said that she didn't have time to explain, and gave a rushed response about the situation.

Alarm bells went off in Bob's head. This shouldn't be happening! He asked her which version of the data she was using for her calculations. It turned out she had been using data from a different project and hadn't realized it. So when all the numbers hadn't added up, she'd suspected fraud or negligence.

If either Bill or Annie had informed the project manager of the issue (as would have been required, so the project manager could capture them in the issue register), then none of this time and frantic effort would have been wasted! Skipping reporting lines can only hurt the project. If the project manager is unaware of an incident, there is no way s/he can even attempt to control it.

Theme three: Quality

> ### Purpose:
>
> **The purpose of the Quality theme is to define and implement the means by which the project will create and verify products that are fit for purpose.**

What this means

The Quality theme expresses the need to collaborate with the customer in defining the quality expectations and measurable acceptance criteria. A full understanding of what is required will help the team plan how they can do their work in order to meet it. Without knowing the "what," planning out the "how" will be impossible. Either too much or too little will be done, and this can lead to many undesired disputes. If too much is done, the costs will seem extravagant. If too little, the project risks non-acceptance with the customer.

The Quality theme goes on to ensure that what has been defined and agreed is actually being built and tested according to the definitions and agreements. Every output is fully defined in a product description, which indicates exactly the minimum criteria the product must meet in order to be acceptable. The project team can then figure out exactly how much work and effort it will take to produce that level of quality. Their plans will reflect that effort and they will manage against those plans. Managing quality then becomes an everyday pursuit: pervasive in every aspect of the project and not just an afterthought.

Illustration

Maria hired Damien, a party planner, to organize her husband's 50th birthday party. She gave him a list of her ideas for the party, which covered the size, theme and type of venue. She felt her ideas were clear, unambiguous and complete. She knew exactly what she wanted. The first thing Damien did, however, was to go through Maria's list with her to ensure that he fully understood her ideas, asking for clarification in measurable terms. The party was to be a black tie event for 300 of their closest friends and family, and held in a five star venue. Once he had fully understood, Damien built his plans to ensure that the quality Maria was asking for was what she would get.

Damien's plans included working with Maria to define specific criteria she required for each element of the party, such as the invitations, decorations, music and menu. Each item was defined in detail, so that when items were purchased or booked for the party they met the exact requirements (the quality criteria). The plans also included quality-checking throughout the project. Each required and defined item needed to be tested. As Maria was busy, she asked her son, Alberto, to be the official tester.

Maria approved the plans, as they showed Damien would be doing the right type and amount of work to create the party she wanted. As agreed in the plans, Alberto did the venue walkthrough before the contract was signed. He did the taste-testing of the menu before it was finalized. He also approved the decorations, the music list and the invitations – all according to the acceptance criteria already defined.

The attention to quality from the start to the end ensured Maria was satisfied with the end result. She was more than happy to sign off her acceptance at the end, and gave Damien a glowing recommendation. Sometimes, a focus on quality can get a bad name as something that is laborious, hard to do, and too slow. Yet, in reality, it is actually less work, easier and faster.

Theme four: Plans

Purpose:
The purpose of the Plans theme is to facilitate communication and control by defining the means of delivering the products (the 'where' and 'how', by whom, and estimating the when and how much).

What this means

PRINCE2® plans are designed and directed at specific audiences. Because there is a potential for three levels of management in a PRINCE2® project management team, there is a potential for three levels of plan for a PRINCE2® project. The top-level plan is the high-level view of the overall project. It's directed at the project board as the key audience, giving them enough information about the current predictions and estimates for the whole project. The second level is for the project manager. It represents a shorter space of time – a stage – within the project, and provides enough detail for the project manager to maintain day-to-day control over the work. Then, if there are team managers on the project management team, they may want and/or be required – as detailed in the terms of the work package – to create a team plan. This plan allows the team manager to stay on top of the work – typically complex in nature, if not in size – carried out by the team members below him/her. Each plan has its own use and, thus, provides just enough information for it.

Illustration

In front of Jo sit three sheets of paper. On them are three different lists representing her plans and goals for running her life. Each list contains a different level of detail to help her manage her time and effort effectively.

The first is her to-do list (i.e. the team plan). After work, she must pick up the dry-cleaning on her way home, meet her friends out for dinner, and leave a message for the neighbor about sweeping his front garden. The level of detail here allows her to execute her tasks for the day with precision and accuracy.

The second sheet is her monthly calendar (i.e. the stage plan). She has listed on it her appointments, meetings and events on the appropriate dates. Most entries are noted with the exact time, such as the 9 am dentist appointment, while others are noted as being a bit more flexible, such as the picnic on Saturday the 16th. The information here allows Jo to manage and control her time on a day-to-day basis.

The final sheet of paper is Jo's list of 100 goals to accomplish before she dies (i.e. the project plan). She has listed things like climbing the pyramids, sailing a boat, seeing the Grand Canyon, swimming with dolphins, etc. She has predicted the year or decade for when she would like to complete each of these goals, as well as listed ideas on how to accomplish them. The level of detail here allows her to manage how and when she will achieve her life goals by showing the major products, activities and resources required.

Theme five: Risk

Purpose:

The purpose of the Risk theme is to identify, assess and control uncertainty and, as a result, improve the ability of a project to succeed.

What this means

Projects cost money. The amount of money they cost is usually compared with the benefits they promise to achieve and the amount of risk they could present. A tricky project decision to make is how much of the project budget should be spent on mitigating risks. The organization's attitude towards risk, the executive's attitude towards risk, and the team's attitude towards risk all need to be included in this consideration. The more money spent on risk-mitigating activities, the less money is then available for getting the project work done. However, if no (or very little) is spent on managing risks, a culture of blame can ensue, with "I told you so" quickly becoming the project motto.

Illustration

Here is a project management conversation overheard from one end of a telephone:

"Yes, you're right. A meteorite may hit the earth and have quite a devastating impact on my project. So, how much of my project budget should I allocate against mitigating the risk that a meteorite may hit the earth?"

... Pause ...

"None, you say? Why's that? If the risk does come to pass, my project may potentially cease to exist. That seems like a pretty big risk to me!"

... Pause ...

"So you're saying it's because of the probability. I must match impact against the probability to gain a true understanding of the size of the risk."

... Pause ...

"I guess you're right. According to NASA and the other powers that be who monitor the skies, the probability is infinitesimal: so small, that even when mapped against the huge impact, the overall size is *very, very low!*"

... Pause ...

"Ok, then. It makes sense that I will not spend one penny managing this risk. I will accept it in full and continue to monitor."

Theme six: Change

Purpose:

The purpose of the Change theme is to identify, assess and control any potential and approved changes to the baseline.

What this means

Just because someone comes up with a great idea halfway through a project – long after the project definition work has been completed and agreed – does not mean we will not include it. However, we will only include changes that make sense. In order to determine if a change makes sense, an assessment must be completed for each and every change request. Based on the assessment, a determination needs to be made by an authorized party within the project management team to include, reject or defer the request. If the decision is to include the change, it must be paid for. This can be from the change budget, additional funding or even at the cost of de-scoping other areas of the project.

Illustration

A client calls the office. The project manager is out. The team member working on the client's product is in. They talk. Though they've met once or twice before at social events, all their project communication tends to go through the project manager, but as previously stated, he's stepped out of the office.

The team member listens to the client and takes on board his request for a "teeny-weeny" change. Since he is already working on the product, it would be no problem for him to add the change. And there it is: scope creep.

It can happen as simply as that; a seemingly small change is requested and accepted without any formal documentation or authorization. It's easy – the team member is currently working on the product, he has all his tools out, and he is finishing things up. A tiny change would be no problem. Or so it seems.

A whole slew of problems can arise from such a transaction. Either that "tiny" change will end up taking the team member five times longer than he expected, or the new change will have knock-on effects on other products, which will then also need to be changed. Another possibility is that the client will forget that s/he requested the change and will not accept the final product because it does not meet the documented requirements. In any of these scenarios, the scope of the project increases without the appropriate time and budget to deal with it being allocated. Even small changes require time and budget expectations to be reset. If there is a change budget to pay for changes, time expectations will still need to be reset.

Theme seven: Progress

Purpose:

The purpose of the Progress theme is to establish mechanisms to monitor and compare actual achievements against those planned; provide a forecast for the project objectives and the project's continued viability; and control any unacceptable deviations.

What this means

Plans are based on estimates, which, by definition, can only be approximations, best judgments or calculations. However, in order to know what activities should be done and when, a plan is usually required. Plans in project management are used as tools to help control the work of the team and as a way to measure the team's progress. Progress information will indicate if the work is going according to plan, or if new or different measures need to be brought in to better control the work.

Just because an estimate – or best guess – in a plan says that an activity will take two days, does not mean it will actually two days. Plans need to be monitored and updated with actual facts and dates in order to determine if the desired and agreed level of progress is happening. Each level of management in the project management team will use the plans as an aid to completing and monitoring work, as well as a tool to help bring unexpected situations back into the agreed timeline.

Illustration

Jessika is working on a fairly large and complex project. One of her team managers is a highly skilled scientist with years of experience. Ten days ago, she authorized a work package to him and he accepted it. Ever since, his team of scientists has been busy at work.

The deadline for the work package is fast approaching and Jessika has no idea if the products will be completed on time. She has no idea because of her own mistake. She decided that regular progress reports (checkpoint reports) were not required for this work package, since she did not have the scientific background to understand the nature of the work. Now, looking in from the outside, all she sees are extremely busy scientists spending hours and hours in labs, working late into the night. Is this what is supposed to be happening? It would have been better to have agreed to some form of progress updates than to live in limbo, waiting and observing frantic behavior that may or may not be normal for this type of work.

A project manager needs to know where the project is at any given time. "Where are we now?" could be the project manager's mantra. Or, even better, "Are we within tolerance?" Progress data from the team managers needs to be captured and compared with the estimates in the plans. Issues need to be captured and assessed against the plans for their impacts. Change control needs to be invoked to assess the impact of changes against the plans.

CHAPTER 4: SEVEN PROCESSES

Process one: Starting up a Project

Purpose:

The purpose of the Starting up a Project process is to ensure that the prerequisites for Initiating a Project are in place by answering the question: do we have a viable and worthwhile project?

The purpose of the Starting up a Project process is as much about preventing poorly conceived projects from ever being initiated as it is about approving the initiation of viable projects.

What this means

To trigger a PRINCE2® project, someone with enough authority from within an organization needs to commission the project idea. The project idea is presented as a project mandate – either formally as a written document, or informally as a verbal request. Regardless of presentation, the idea is still just an idea. Even if it is a wonderful idea, it may be that it is not possible to execute – perhaps due to the organization's existing time and resources, or because it's not sustainable, or maybe because business conditions have changed and the idea is no longer valid. The Starting up a Project process ensures that bad ideas are not pursued and good ideas are understood before they are initiated.

The project board will need information about the project idea before they commit resources to its initiation. A high-level investigation will determine answers to these basic questions about the project's viability, logistics and resource commitment.

Illustration

A group of old friends meet up in a pub. They sit around a table, catching up on each others' lives. They realize how much they miss each other, and start talking about spending more time together. Someone invariably suggests going on holiday together. The gang, together again, rally round the idea. Already, they are talking about the best times of the year to go, and where to travel.

Promises are made, but not kept. Some friends won't be able to afford it. Some won't get the time off work. Others, still keen on the idea, won't be able to agree on the basics – such as the type of holiday (i.e. the business options), or whether to use a travel agent or book it themselves (i.e. the project approach).

Just because someone has an idea doesn't mean it's a good one. Just because it sounds like a good idea in theory doesn't mean it will last the test of time. Ideas need to be poked at, tested, reviewed and considered. If they are worthy and viable, they can be pursued in earnest. If not, they'll do it all over again at the next pub meet-up.

Process two: Directing a Project

Purpose: *The purpose of the Directing a Project process is to enable the project board to be accountable for the project's success by making key decisions and exercising overall control while delegating day-to-day management of the project to the project manager.*

What this means

Directing a Project is a process reserved for the project board. In this process, project board members make scheduled and unscheduled decisions. Their scheduled key decisions are made at the start of the project, at the end of the project, and at the end of each delivery stage. Their unscheduled decisions are normally made at times where the project manager is forecast to exceed his/her tolerances, as laid down by the board. They can also be at any other time. Board members are allowed to pick up the phone, e-mail, or communicate otherwise with the project manager at any point in time. This is called "giving ad hoc direction." It is advisable for the project manager to record such ad hoc direction in writing – possibly via e-mail – so that the content and its significance is not later misconstrued or devalued.

Illustration

As Jim approached Fred in the corridor leading to the open-plan office, Fred had an overwhelming sense of dread.

However, it wasn't until Jim started talking that Fred truly understood this odd emotional reaction.

"Fred, I'm glad I caught you. I've just been asked to take on this project and, when I was thinking of who could be the project manager, I immediately thought of you. You are perfect for this."

Jim spoke on and on in elated tones. Fred stopped listening. He'd been here before. In fact, three times before. When Jim's enthusiasm reached a feverish pitch, Fred snapped.

"As long as it won't be like before!" he almost yelled in a very loud, stern tone.

"Huh? Uh, what do you mean?" Jim responded, completely stunned.

"Well, let's see," Jim continued, as he regained his composure. "The last three projects on which we 'worked together,' I was left completely on my own … "

(Authorize initiation – confirm that all members have agreed roles.)

" … One was a complete disaster, and only stopped when Maria (the internal legal consultant) advised the corporate management team of the nebulous legal grey areas we were fast approaching … "

(Authorize the project – confirm that there has been a review of the risks.)

" … The second finished all right, but I am now not on speaking terms with over half of the customer service department … "

(Authorize project closure – ensure that the appropriate groups have been made aware of their responsibility for taking any recommended actions forward.)

" … And the third technically finished six months ago, but the client just called me asking for my latest progress report."

(Authorize project closure – review and issue a project closure notification.)

"So, if you really want me to project-manage this new project, I need things to be different. I'm all for the Management by Exception principle – it lets me get on with my job without being micromanaged – but 'management by complete and utter absence' is not fair. It's not fair to me, the team or the customer! If you can accept my terms, then I'm on board, but if you can't, then you'll need to find someone else."

"I'll let you think about it," added Fred, confident things would be fine. He returned to his desk and updated his daily log with notes on their conversation, just in case.

Process three: Initiating a Project

Purpose:
The purpose of the Initiating a Project process is to establish solid foundations for the project, enabling the organization to understand the work that needs to be done to deliver the project's products before committing to a significant spend.

What this means

If a project is to progress smoothly, it needs to have certain criteria defined upfront, an agreed set of rules to abide by, and a plan to work against. The Initiating a Project process puts these details in place by focusing the time and attention of the project management team on deciding and agreeing to the terms of the project before the actual specialist or technical work begins. If the terms and conditions can be agreed, then there is a better chance of them being adhered to during the actual work. If there are issues or concerns with agreeing the terms, then the specialist work should not commence until these have been negotiated and finalized. There is nothing worse than starting a project under the pretence that "we" will figure it out as we go. That only leads to disaster and, more likely, strained relations with everyone involved. There will no longer be a "we," just an "us" and a "them," even after the project dies a painful death.

Illustration

Salima pulled out her stage plan for the initiation stage and began to laugh. When she had first started using PRINCE2® several years back, she had the false impression that the initiation stage was all about the project manager busily documenting a bunch of bureaucratic documents for the sake of bureaucratically documenting documents. If only the "Salima of a few years back" could see her initiation stage plan today. How eye-opening it would have been.

Salima's schedule had her attending meetings, running workshops, conducting presentations, delegating pieces of work, checking on progress, reviewing drafts, and even producing a bit of documentation. It takes a lot of input, negotiation, facilitation, persuasion and – in some cases – mediation, for the project management team to establish the foundations for the project. Although the project manager is responsible for producing much of the documentation in the Initiating a Project process, s/he must work with a lot of other resources to get it right.

In her case, Salima was working with an entire team of expert users to help her define the quality criteria for all the products that were being planned for. She was also holding planning workshops with team managers to ensure that their input and expertise was being considered, as well as to confirm their availability and commitment to carry out the team manager role. She was having regular meetings with project assurance to review the information sets being defined for the project. She even had a few presentations to deliver to key stakeholders, in order to maintain their level of support and interest in the project.

All of these activities were planned for in the initiation stage plan and authorized by the project board in the "authorize initiation" step *(see Chapter 6)*. Everyone on the project board realized that this amount of effort was required to define the project and garner support and agreement. The project initiation documentation (PID) resulting from this stage will form the "contract" between Salima and her project board. It is in everyone's best interest that this is done correctly: with the right levels of involvement from the right resources at the right times.

Process four: Controlling a Stage

Purpose:

The purpose of the Controlling a Stage process is to assign work to be done, monitor such work, deal with issues, report progress to the project board and take corrective actions to ensure that the stage remains within tolerance.

What this means

Just as an orchestra's conductor is authorized to conduct and direct a musical piece (not the complete works) of a composer, a project manager is authorized to manage a stage (not the entire project) on behalf of the project board. In keeping with this analogy, the orchestral conductor has the music sheets in front of him/her, assisting the aid of his/her direction to the appropriate musicians and their instruments. The project manager uses the stage plan and work packages to steer the work of the team managers. And finally, the conductor of an orchestra – as the group's focal point – not only directs the music, but handles the issues (personality conflicts, for example) and wards off the risks (of mistakes). The project manager uses the risk and issues registers to help control the stage.

Illustration

Mark is the project manager. He sees himself as a spoke in the wheel. The flow of information up and down the project goes through him. This is how Mark remains in control. He takes direction from the project board and delegates work out to team managers. When team managers have issues, they raise them with Mark. If those issues are indeed exceptions (exceeding stage-level tolerances), then Mark escalates them to the board.

Before Mark started the stage, his stage plan was reviewed, examined and authorized by the project board. The project board was fully aware of the products and activities Mark intended to handle, and approved him for them. Mark uses this stage plan on a daily basis to instruct him on what to do next. Some days, he needs to authorize work packages; other days he needs to review progress and send highlight reports. As his current stage is drawing to an end, he has noticed that soon he will need to start planning the next stage (via the Managing a Stage Boundary process). Today, however, he is to review his risk and issue registers. He is chairing the risk workshop in the morning, in which the risk owners and risk actionees will report their progress and brainstorm further ideas. Later in the day, he has reserved time with the project support team to review and update the statuses of several recent issues that have been resolved.

Process five: Managing Product Delivery

Purpose:

The purpose of the Managing Product Delivery process is to control the link between the project manager and the team manager(s), by placing formal requirements on accepting, executing and delivering project work.

What this means

Project managers may be good at managing projects, but they don't necessarily have the skills to do the specialist work on it; hence, the need for the team manager role. Team managers have the requisite skill set to do or manage the specialist work. Depending on the size and nature of the project, there may be several team managers working on different aspects or products for the project. However, if the project is small in nature or size *and* the project manager also has the requisite specialist skills, there may be no need for additional people to fulfill the team manager role. Regardless of the situation, the work must still be agreed on, executed and handed back to the project. The mechanics of how this is done must be agreed in the work package. Beyond that, the mechanics of the specialist work is left to the specialists under their agreed terms and conditions.

Illustration

Question: Who's a better project manager?

Jacques used to be a high-level techie, and was able to find solutions where no one else was. He works hard, learns all the latest methods, has all the latest gadgets, and is always willing to stay late to help finish tasks. He has always been a significant asset to any project team.

Jackie has never been a techie. She knows people, however. She's supervised and managed up to hundreds of staff members through times of recession, expansions, mergers and downsizes. She is excellent at managing people through change, as well as getting the most out of them.

The answer to the question is: it depends. However, it does not depend on if the project is technical in nature. The best project manager knows how to manage. The name is in the title; a project manager will allow a team manager and team members to get on with the specialist work, stepping in only to help them manage the work, not do it.

If Jacques, as project manager, steps in to help bring the team back on track by doing techie tasks, he is taking his eyes off the project he is supposed to be managing, and repositioning himself as a team member. If the team is falling behind, Jacques, as project manager, will need to help manage the situation: remove obstacles, find opportunities, resources and answers.

However, if Jackie is clueless about the technical nature of the project, and can only manage the situation, she might be relying on specialists who take her project down a path that is unrecoverable. If she allows the specialists full reign over all the decisions – and doesn't understand the impacts of them – she may lock the project and/or the business into solutions that are not sustainable.

Process six: Managing a Stage Boundary

Purpose:

The purpose of the Managing a Stage Boundary process is to enable the project board to be provided with sufficient information by the project manager, so that it can review the success of the current stage, approve the next stage plan, review the updated project plan, and confirm continued business justification and acceptability of the risks. Therefore, the process should be executed at, or close to the end of, each management stage.

> **Projects do not always go to plan and in response to an exception report (if the stage or project is forecast to exceed its tolerances) the project board may request that the current stage (and possibly the project) is re-planned. The output from re-planning is an exception plan which is submitted for project board approval in the same way that a stage plan is submitted for approval.**

What this means

After each stage completion, the project board will make a key decision about the project. Either they will continue to fund the project by authorizing the next stage, or they will request a premature close. In order to make such a monumental decision, the project board requires up-to-date and accurate information. Without it, they could potentially make the wrong decision. Therefore, it is important for the project manager to gather the most up-to-date information about the project, its progress and its continued viability. Once it has been presented to them, the project board members will be able to make the appropriate and informed decision that best suits the needs and interests of the business, the users and the suppliers. Similarly, if the project board requests that the stage or project be re-planned based on an exception situation, the project manager will need to present the most up-to-date information about the project, especially about the impact of the exception on the project.

Illustration

In the film *Austin Powers: International Man of Mystery* (1997), Dr Evil, a villain who had been cryogenically frozen for 30 years, unfreezes and wants to hold the world hostage in an evil plot for the sum of one million dollars! Thirty years is a long time to go without information. The world changes so quickly these days; six months can be a long time to go without information.

The project board will get to decide how far into the future they want to go before they stop and assess and decide if they want to continue with a project or not. At each of these stopping points – often called "end-stage assessments" – they will need up-to-date and accurate information about the current situation as it currently stands – not from six months ago, for example, when the original business case and project plan was written. Thus, the project manager is tasked with researching and gathering this data towards the end of every stage in the Managing a Stage Boundary process. Of course, the project board will receive regular highlight reports detailing the progress of a stage during its execution, but the end-stage assessment concerns more than just progress. It is a full assessment of the progress made to date, but also includes revised predictions for the future and a confirmation of continued viability – all of which is required to determine whether to carry on with the project or to stop.

Process seven: Closing a Project

Purpose:

The purpose of the Closing a Project process is to provide a fixed point at which acceptance for the project product is confirmed, and to recognize that objectives set out in the original project initiation documentation have been achieved (or approved changes to the objectives have been

---

> **achieved), or that the project has nothing more to contribute.**

What this means

After a project ends, most of the project management team members will move on to other projects or back to their old jobs. Regardless of where they move on to, they leave the project in their past. If users have questions about the project's products after a project has closed, it is often difficult to find anyone who had worked on the project to ask. Even if they could be found, it would be unlikely that they would remember enough of the details and intricacies to be able to answer a usability question.

One of the major objectives of the Closing a Project process is to ensure that users are provided with all the relevant information available to use, operate and maintain the project's products. If a usability question arises after the project has finished, they will be able to answer it themselves. Additionally, this process ensures that the project has not only passed on ownership of the outputs, but also the lessons from the effort (i.e. the lessons report), the completed documentation of what actually happened (i.e. the complete, updated and archived documentation) and a complete assessment of the effort and its success (i.e. the end project report).

Illustration

At Janie's previous company, there wasn't really a process to properly close down a project. When they were done with the specialist products, they would turn off the old version and turn on the new one. There was always a long list of new project ideas to be started. The pressure to quickly (and sloppily) hand over the current project outputs and start working on the new ones was immense. Senior management at her old firm knew this was a problem, but continued to support the lack of any proper handover process in order to keep moving forward with new product creation.

The results of this approach were disastrous. The users were unhappy with the products. Because the users either didn't use the products or misused them, the benefits that had justified the project were not realized. As Janie was the project manager who introduced the new outputs, her name was associated with them. She received endless phone calls from the operational teams asking how to maintain or manage different outputs. With the high-speed turnaround of projects, rarely did she remember the specifics of any one output among the many she churned out.

When Janie joined her new company, she was elated to hear that the use of PRINCE2® was embedded in the organization. When planning for the final delivery stage of her project, Janie relished the opportunity to finally plan it and do it right. She looked forward to being able to review a final product status account to confirm that the project's products had been approved and met their quality criteria. She couldn't wait to confirm acceptance from operations and maintenance organizations, and transfer the responsibilities for the products to them. She was excited to finally do a proper evaluation of a completed project: to review the original and current version of the project initiation documentation, assess the project against the expected benefits in the business case, and review the team performance. And lastly, she was delighted by the idea of working with the project management team to prepare a lessons report, in which she would reflect on the experience and really learn from what had gone well and what had gone badly.

CHAPTER 5: STARTING UP A PROJECT

Appoint the executive and the project manager

Description:

To get anything done in the project, a decision maker with appropriate authority is needed – the executive – who represents the interest of the business stakeholder(s). The appointment of the executive is a prerequisite to ensuring that the project is justified.

The appointment of a project manager allows for the project to be managed on a day-to-day basis on behalf of the executive. The executive may need to consult with, and gain agreement from, corporate or program management when appointing a project manager.

What this means

To get the project idea off the ground, a member of management with enough seniority, interest and authority will need to be appointed. This person will own the project, but will rarely have enough time to dedicate to doing it. Therefore, s/he will appoint a project manager. The project manager will do the legwork. They will research the idea and work with stakeholders amongst others (including the executive) to gather high-level information on which a decision to start the project or not can be based. The project manager should be trusted by the executive, as his/her skills will be required to bring the project to successful completion – adding yet another triumph to the name and reputation of the executive.

Illustration

James was tapped on the shoulder by his boss and asked to sponsor the project idea just announced at the company meeting. Understanding that he was taking on the role of the project board executive and accepting total accountability for the project, James turned around and tapped Julia on the shoulder, asking her to be the project manager. Having worked on several projects before in the past, James and Julia were comfortable taking on these roles. James's role description was produced by the corporate management team above him. Once he had gained a firm understanding of his authority levels as an executive on the project, James could advise Julia on where her authority levels below him would lie. She then drew up her role description with these limits in mind.

Although this was a small project within the overall organization, it was important for James and Julia to document the differences between their roles. James would be the decision maker for the project, and Julia the planner and doer. This clear line of authority was now not only clear to them, but also to all the stakeholders affected by the project work. James could spend his time managing his directorate, promoting the project idea and advising Julia. Julia could spend her time getting on with managing the project, stage by stage.

Capture previous lessons

Description:

A number of lessons may have been learned by other projects, corporate or program management, and external organizations about weaknesses or strengths of the processes, procedures, techniques and tools used, when they were used, how they were used and by whom.

What this means

Although you might have just been presented with a seemingly brilliant idea about the future, one of the first activities should be to look back into the past. Imperative questions need to be asked and answered before taking the idea any further. Has anything like this project ever been attempted before? If so, what can we learn from that experience? What went well that we could repeat? And what mistakes were made that we can avoid? If nothing like this has been done before, why not? Did others think of it and decided not pursue it? What was their reasoning? What threats did they foresee that we might be missing? Can we address those threats and still turn this into a positive experience?

Illustration

Considerations are being made to include a visitor centre in the terminal building in PortCity during their next big refurbishment project. Never having been involved in setting up or even managing a visitor centre, no one in the organization could provide any insight into how best to go about doing it. One of the administrator's old neighbors had worked at the Hall of Justice in RiverCity a few years back, when they opened their visitor centre. The project manager looked the neighbor up and met with them to discuss his experiences. The project manager asked the neighbor what went well during the project and what he would have done differently if he had had the chance to do it over again. From this interview, the project manager gathered several key ideas on how best to go about the project, where the risky areas might be, and possible starting points.

The neighbor gave the name and number of someone who had helped him when he started his project. This second contact was also from PortCity, and potentially had even more information and lessons learned about the local clientele, public reactions and climate. Although the RiverCity project went well, the dynamics could have been different in PortCity, so another interview was set up.

Design and appoint the project management team

Description:

The project needs the right people in place, with the authority, responsibility and knowledge to make decisions in a timely manner. The project management team needs to reflect the interests of all parties who will be involved, including business, user and supplier interests.

It is essential for a well-run project that every individual involved in the management of the project understands and agrees who is accountable to whom for what, who is responsible for what, and what the reporting and communication lines are.

What this means

For very small, simple projects, many of the PRINCE2®
roles can be combined, reducing the need for a large
number of people in a situation that does not call for it. For
example, the executive and senior user, who both come
from the customer organization, can often be combined.
Additionally, the project manager can fulfill the roles of
project support and team manager. However, the larger or
more complex a project is, the more need there will be for
more people to be involved. Some roles may even need to
be shared by more than one person (for example, there
could be more than one senior user, multiple team
managers and a project support team). However, for the
roles of executive and project manager, there should only
ever be one person.

Illustration

Duane and Birthe worked together on a small project. After
they had reviewed lessons from previous small projects,
they realized they could combine roles for theirs. Previous
projects, to which a lot of people had been added, ended up
being slower and less efficient than other projects for which
the team had been kept to an absolute minimum.

Duane then planned to fulfill three roles: those of the
project manager, the team manager and the project support.
He would not have to assign himself work packages, nor
create team plans, but he would have to switch between
focusing on how the stage was progressing and focusing on
specialist work at hand. He would also have to be very
diligent in maintaining his own administration.

Birthe planned to tackle both the roles of executive and senior user, as well as retain both business and user assurance responsibilities. She appointed a senior supplier from the supplier organization to fulfill the roles of senior supplier and supplier assurance. Birthe could have informal project board meetings via phone and e-mails with the senior supplier, whenever needed. To satisfy her assurance roles, Birthe arranged to hold regular mentoring and review meetings with Duane. And finally, Duane and Birthe split the change authority role – with Duane taking authority on all changes worth up to £500, and Birthe taking the authority for anything worth more than £500. Their design was documented in an e-mail, and the role descriptions were filed in a project folder.

Prepare the outline business case

> ### Description:
>
> *When setting up, and particularly while running the project, it is all too easy to concentrate on what is being done and how it is to be done, while ignoring why it needs to be done. The business case states why the work is worth doing and, as such, is a crucial element of the project.*
>
> *Given the information available, the outline business case is likely to be only a high-level view at this time. It proves an agreed foundation for a more extensive business case developed in the Initiating a Project process.*

What this means

The executive should be drafting the outline business case, especially capturing information about objectives, reasons, expected benefits, and costs associated with the project idea. Meanwhile, the project manager will be consulting with the executive and the senior user to capture early opinions and ideas about the expectations and acceptance criteria associated with the project idea. He/she should also be capturing any risks associated with these findings on the daily log. Because it's only early days with the idea, there may not be much detailed knowledge available. Only enough information to formulate a decision about the project idea's viability is required (this depending on the project idea concerned).

Illustration

Based on your own experience, expertise and understanding of the following, decide, at a high level, if these are good or bad ideas:

- Creating a company website
- Upgrading the existing IT infrastructure
- Changing working practices of the front-line staff
- Conducting a staff audit
- Moving company headquarters to a different building
- Outsourcing the company help desk overseas.

Depending on your situation, you may or may not be able to make a case for one or more of these actions. If you cannot make a case, even at a high level, you should not start the project.

Select the project approach and assemble the project brief

Description:

Before any planning of the project can be done, decisions must be made regarding how the work of the project is going to be approached ... An agreed project brief ensures that the project has a commonly understood and well-defined start point.

What this means

A project brief is just that: brief. Although there are several key sections to consider and possibly document, the overall aim is to keep it as brief as possible. The project brief is created during the pre-project preparation and, thus, is only an early opportunity to explore the idea later to be presented in the project mandate at a high level. At a high level, a feasible way to execute the project needs to be found: one that still provides the users with an acceptable end product, while giving the business enough benefits to make it worthwhile.

Illustration

A husband and wife are considering how best to go about a DIY project (what approach to use). Jason believes that, if he wants something done right, he should do it himself. Jason has some limited experience in crafting things from scratch. He not only has a clear vision of what he wants, but the drive and determination to complete what he starts. He also has the time to do it, which counts as free labor for this project.

Meghan, his wife, doesn't quite agree. She feels that, if you want quality work done, you must pay professionals to do it. Her experiences and previous lessons tell her that Jason's perceptions of his own craftwork are not quite the same as hers. She either has to live with taps installed backwards, walls painted the wrong color, and doors that open out instead of in, or pay someone to fix them after Jason has finished. She would rather use professionals from the start – ones who can utilize their years of experience and possibly some sort of a qualification or degree. Not only will they get what they want, but it will be exactly right the first time.

Together, Meghan and Jason took time out to evaluate their options. They considered other changes that were going on in and around their household, such as the impending birth of their first child and the major road works going on in their neighborhood. They considered the quality standards they would want the DIY project to meet, and the safety and security constraints that would be required with the new baby. At the end of the discussion, they agreed to hire in professionals. The cost/time/risk assessment of this option proved it was the best approach for delivering the desired outputs, as well as achieving the outline business case. Once agreed, they could then assemble the project brief.

Plan the initiation stage

Description:
Initiating a Project takes time and consumes resources. The work should be planned and approved like any other project work. This also ensures that the initiation is not aimless and unstructured.

What this means

The work and effort required to create and document the project initiation documentation needs to be planned out. The plan for this initial stage should be at a stage plan level, allowing the project manager to maintain day-to-day control over it. Typical activities shown in the plan may include such things as workshops, meetings, drafts, consultations and reviews. All of these will need to be funded and resourced. The only way the project board can allocate enough time and resources for this stage is if it is clearly presented in the plan.

Illustration

Sean (the project manager) and Julie (the executive) were in a rush. Thus far, they had informally discussed all the aspects of the small project idea. In their dialog, they felt that they had exhausted the activities outlined in the Starting up a Project process. Sean believed he was ready to move to the Initiating a Project process. Julie gave him the nod to proceed. The only thing missing from their conversation was the detail about how the initiation stage would be run. Sean assumed he would fit the initiation stage work around his other business as usual duties. Julie believed that he would drop everything in order to complete the initiation. After a week, Julie expected Sean to return with at least a draft of the PID, so they could pick up their conversations about the project and start agreeing on some of the basics. When she called him in, it turned out he hadn't even started.

Even in a very informal performance of the Starting up a Project process, it is important to agree on the time, money, effort and resources required to do the next step, the initiation stage.

CHAPTER 6: DIRECTING A PROJECT

Authorize initiation

Description:

Projects take time and cost money to initiate, so the activities for initiation should be planned, monitored and controlled. The project board activity to authorize initiation ensures that such investment is worthwhile.

What this means

Decision: Is this project idea worthy of further investigation?

Once an idea that is at least worthy of a second (more detailed) look has been discovered, a request will be sent to the project board to authorize initiation. This decision publicly shows commitment to the organization and other senior managers. In essence, the project board is saying, "This idea has been deemed worthy of further investigation. If the project manager comes around to bother you or your staff, it probably has to do with this project, and s/he has our permission." By making this decision, the project board does not commit itself to the entire project, as only a few key pieces of information have been researched to date. However, through their public commitment to resourcing the stage plan for initiation, they demonstrate their enthusiasm for the initial findings thus far.

Illustration

How do you know if you have enough information to determine if the idea for a project is worthwhile? In 1962, Decca Records didn't think the Beatles had the right sound for the times. In 1977, Digital Equipment Corporation didn't feel that there would be enough people interested in having a personal computer in their homes. In 1999, Excite didn't see the value of buying Google for one million pounds.

These, of course, were famous bad business decisions that turned out to be wrong ones. Taking these decisions is difficult. PRINCE2® allows monumental decisions like these to be broken into. To help prioritize work, gain clarity, and understand total commitment and investment, the decision to commit to a project is made in two steps. The first is to decide to investigate further, rather than rely on high-level information. Once the investigation has been completed and the details sorted, then another decision can be taken to commit to the project (*see Chapter 6, Authorize the project*).

How different the world would look if all major investment decisions were approached like this! Western Union might have bought the telephone patent for £100,000. Atari or Hewlett-Packard might have hired Steve Jobs and Steve Wozniak without their college degrees, instead of competing against them. And The Coca-Cola Company may have purchased the then-bankrupt competitor and rival Pepsi in 1931.

Authorize the project

Description:

This activity will be triggered by a request from the project manager for authorization to deliver the project, and should be performed in parallel with authorizing a stage or exception plan. The objective of authorizing the project is to decide whether to proceed with the rest of the project.

What this means

Decision: Now that we see it in detail, do we really and truly believe in this project idea?

The completed PID will contain all the details of what the project is to achieve, who will be involved, how it will be run and managed, and why it is needed in the first place. Using the PID as an objective tool, the project board will then need to decide if they are still committed to the idea. Now that they see it in detail, will they publicly commit to the project for a second time? This time, their decision will indicate to the rest of the organization and other key stakeholders that the project idea is now not only viable and worthwhile, but desirable and achievable.

Illustration

Carlos – the project board executive – was, along with the rest of his board, about to take the decision to authorize a project. This project was to be the biggest their company had ever taken on in its history. The project board had previously agreed, in principle, to the project through an informal onsite meeting (***authorize initiation***), but now was the time to declare commitment and investment, or prematurely close it down.

To eliminate distractions, Carlos hosted an offsite meeting with the project board members, where they could review, discuss and approve the project, or not. He wanted the decision they made to be the right one. Carlos also insisted, as a prerequisite for attending the meeting, that all project board members and/or their designated project assurance resources had reviewed and assessed the project's lesson log, PID and benefits review plan. If they were to discuss this project in detail, the details had to be known and understood beforehand.

For where there were contentious areas – especially between the senior users and the senior suppliers – rational discussions were held, negotiations – where necessary – were made, and resolutions were found at the senior management level. As a result of this meeting, the common level of understanding and deep level of commitment that Carlos sought was achieved. This fundamental point in the project would set the precedence for the level of engagement required from the project board for this specific project. When the decision was made at the end of the day, they were all certain it was the right one.

Authorize a stage or exception plan

Description:

It is important that a stage starts only when the project board says it should. The project board authorizes a management stage by reviewing the performance of the current stage and approving the stage plan for the next stage. Approval of stage plans occurs at the end of every management stage except the last one.

If an exception has occurred during the stage, the project board may request that the project manager produces an exception plan for project board approval.

What this means

Decision: Do we stop here, or continue on?

Even though the project board has authorized the project in a separate decision, they only agree to commit to funding and resourcing the project one stage at a time. At the end of each stage, they must again agree to continue or to prematurely close it down. In order to make such key decisions, the project board requires up-to-date and accurate information from the project manager. An updated project plan and business case will prove the project is still worthwhile and achievable. The next stage plan will show the details of the next proposed work needing funding and resources. And finally, the end-stage report proves that the current stage has been successfully completed, and the team is ready to move on to the next stage.

If the project board is meeting to review an exception plan, then it was they who requested to see one. When a project manager is predicting to exceed his/her stage-level tolerances, then s/he must first raise an exception report. The report explains the situation and provides a number of options, including the project manager's recommended one. As long as the situation does not take the project board outside of project-level tolerances, they are free to make any decision they wish. They could fix the problem for the project manager, they could request the project prematurely close, or they could request to see an exception plan. Usually, the project board will want to see one of the options suggested from the exception report in more detail in the exception plan (hopefully the recommended option). If requested through the "give ad hoc direction" action, then the project manager uses the Managing a Stage Boundary process. S/he would create the exception plan, update the project plan and business case, and document an end-stage report providing an assessment of the stage up to the point of the exception situation. This information would then be used to assess whether to continue with the project or not. Like at the natural end of a stage, the project board uses this up-to-date information to determine if the project, at this point, is worth continued investment to recover from the exception or if they should prematurely close it down.

Illustration

Deborah's project was almost complete. She had one more scheduled stage to do, which mainly focused on adding nice-to-have functionality to her existing project's products. She had just performed the Managing a Stage Boundary process, in preparation for the end-stage assessment with the project board. The board held these meetings in person to provide a specific time and space to hash out any concerns and answer questions before authorizing a stage. In this particular meeting, where Deborah wanted the final stage to be authorized, the project board was divided. Some members wanted to cut and run, while the others wanted to stick it out to the end. For the ones wishing to end prematurely, the last stage did not convince them as being worth the effort. The sooner the project resources could be released back to their business as usual, the better; in their opinion, the project had gone on long enough. However, other members wanted to continue to the end to give the team the satisfaction of completing the effort. By cutting them off before the end, it might destroy or severely damage their morale. In the end, the decision was made by the executive, who limited the discussions after everyone had had their chance to voice their opinions. He decided to continue as planned for the final stage.

Give ad hoc direction

Description:

Project board members may offer informal guidance or respond to requests for advice at any time during a project. The need for consultation between the project managers and the project board is likely to be particularly frequent during the initiation stage and when approaching stage boundaries.

Ad hoc direction may be given collectively or by individual project board members.

6: Directing a Project

What this means

Decision: Do I/we pick up the phone to the project manager (or e-mail, smoke signal, Morse code him, etc.) and give solicited and/or unsolicited advice?

If the project board, or even just a member of the board, is communicating with the project manager outside of the end-stage assessments, they are performing the "give ad hoc direction" action. They may do this because the project manager has requested some advice, or because the project board member(s) has/have a question for the project manager. Either way, it always a good idea to record these ad hoc conversations, e-mails, or phone calls and their results.

Illustration

Will, the senior user, stopped Katerina in the hallway with a question about the project she was managing. The following day, Naomi, the project board executive, e-mailed Katerina. Later on, she received a phone call from the senior supplier, asking for a quick clarification of the highlight report.

Although all of these communications with the project board members were on informal terms, Katerina kept a record of each of them in her daily log and, where appropriate, in the project documentation too. The senior user's question was really a request for change on one of the existing products, and Katerina started the change control procedure by capturing it on the issue register. The executive's e-mail was really an update on a threat that she owned. Katerina updated the risk register and continued with the risk management procedure. The five-minute explanation to the senior supplier was only noted on her daily log. Although it only took five minutes, this was the third time it had happened. If a trend was to arise from this, she may solicit informal advice about a potential change to the communication channel through which the senior supplier receives his highlight reports.

Authorize project closure

Description:

The controlled close of a project is as important as the controlled start. There must be a point when the objectives set out in the original and current versions of the project initiation documentation and project plan are assessed ... Without this approach, the project may never end; a project can become business as usual and the original focus on the benefits will be lost.

What this means

Decision: Is it over?

It's not over until the project board says it's over. The project board will want to see evidence before confirming the project closure – evidence that the products have been completed, tested and approved; evidence that the products, remaining issues, risks and the benefits review plan have all been handed over; and evidence that the project has been evaluated and lessons learned and shared.

Illustration

All that was left for Joaquin to do now was to click "send" on the project closure notification e-mail to his project stakeholder. He had received the draft project closure recommendation from Evie, the project manager, confirming that the project was ready to close. The project assurance resources had helped him review and assess the project initiation documentation, the end project report, the lessons report and the benefits review plan. The project had delivered its objectives and had nothing left to contribute. Any ideas for future enhancements (follow-on action recommendations) for future projects or continual improvement efforts were captured and shared with the appropriate groups. The handover of the project's products was successful and deemed sustainable. The business case had been scrutinized, reconciling the expected costs with the actual costs and identifying which benefits had actually materialized and which were still to be realized. The arrangements for resourcing the remaining benefits listed in the benefits review plan had been confirmed and agreed.

As the executive – the ultimate decision maker on the project – Joaquin did it. He hit send. Project stakeholders were then informed they could withdraw their support and infrastructure resources, as well as notified of the closing date for costs to be charged against the project.

CHAPTER 7: INITIATING A PROJECT

Prepare the risk management strategy

Description:

The risk management strategy describes the goals of applying risk management, the procedure that will be adopted, the roles and responsibilities, the risk tolerances, the timing of risk management activities, the tools and techniques that will be used, and the reporting requirements.

What this means

Consideration: How will this project team manage risks?

The project management team needs to decide how they want to manage risks before they can start to manage them on the project. Each project will be different, not only because of the people involved, but the size and nature of the project. Some organizations will have strict risk management guidelines, while others may not have any. Additionally, partnership projects will need to investigate the best method for the project: theirs, ours, or a combination of the two?

Sample considerations:

- How risk-averse is the organization and the project board?

- How will risk management be delegated throughout the project management team?
- How will risks be captured? In a Microsoft® Excel® spreadsheet or a database?
- How will risks be analyzed and assessed? Using a risk model or software?
- How will risks be rated? What scales will determine a "high," "medium" or "low" rating?
- How often should risks be reviewed and reported?
- How will the team respond to risks? Using PRINCE2® responses or corporate standards?
- How much risk are they willing to live with?
- How much money should be set aside to deal with risks?

Illustration

Tommy reviewed the corporate risk management strategy for the construction company he worked for. Most of the risks and the guidance related to catastrophic risks, health and safety standards and regulatory guidance. Tommy's project was about hiring a design firm to launch a new marketing campaign. Nothing in the existing corporate documentation mentioned risks regarding advertising, reputation or commerciality. Tommy would have to start almost from scratch to create the project's risk management strategy.

As a result of working with the project board, members of the project assurance team, and the design firm, Tommy's end result was a well-prepared and somewhat cautious strategy. The project board's appetite for risk was fairly low, so they set the risk tolerance levels for the project quite low. Based on that decision, Tommy put a strict risk management procedure in place and recommended a fairly large risk budget. Risks were to be reviewed twice weekly by the project manager and project support. Weekly risk reports were to be provided to the project board and the design firm's senior management team. Project assurance was to perform monthly reviews of the procedures. A quarterly audit was scheduled to ensure adequate risk management in accordance with the strategy.

Prepare the configuration management strategy

Description:

Configuration management is essential for the project to maintain control over its management and specialist products. The level of control required will vary from project to project. The maximum level of control possible is determined by breaking down the project's products until the level is reached at which a component can be independently installed, replaced or modified. However, the level of control exercise will be influenced by the importance of the project and the complexity of the relationship between its products.

What this means

Considerations: How will this project team manage its configuration? And how will this project team control change?

The project management team needs to decide how they want to manage the project's configuration before they can start to manage it. Each project will be different – not only because of the people involved, but the size and nature of the project. Some organizations will have strict configuration management and change control guidelines, while others may not have any. Additionally, partnership projects will need to investigate the best method for this project: theirs, ours, or a combination of the two?

Sample considerations:

- How will configuration management activities be performed on this project, and by whom?
- How will change control activities be performed on this project, and by whom?
- How will records be kept, stored and accessed?
- How will issues and changes be captured?
- How often will records be reviewed, audited and reported?
- How often will configuration management and change control activities be performed?
- How will configuration management be delegated throughout the project management team?
- How – if needed – will the change authority function of the project board be delegated within the project management team?
- How will issues and change be prioritized?
- How much money will be set aside to manage change?
- How will decisions on changes (requests for change and off-specifications) be made?

Illustration

In deciding how they were going to manage the project's configuration, Sandra and her team had to define their procedures for configuration management. They were lucky that their organization – the International Management Journal Network (IMJN) – had clear and well-defined procedures in place for projects that had documents as their main outputs. From years of doing projects that produced recommendation papers, research articles and case studies, the organization had developed excellent tools and techniques to identify, track and protect documents, these ranging from draft forms to final versions.

Sandra's project was to design and host a massive marketing event to coincide with their company's upcoming 10-year anniversary. Some of the products that were to result from the project did include some documents, such as the invitations, guest list, seating chart and contracts with suppliers. These could follow the organization's current configuration management standards. However, a lot of the products for the project would include things such as marketing gadgets and giveaways for their guests. Decisions needed to be made on how to identify these gadgets and gizmos, where to store them, and how to protect them against theft or damages until the big day. Storing these physical products on the company's document management system would not be appropriate.

In the end, Sandra and her team cleared out a space in one of the company's storage cupboards in the basement. When the physical products were completed and delivered to the site, they were stored under lock and key until they were needed at the event itself. A record system ("configuration item records") was devised to identify the different decorations (banners, signs, balloons and booths) and giveaways (pens, toys, t-shirts, digital clocks, magnets, handheld tablets, smart phones and memory sticks). These records also helped manage the relationships between the different products – for example, the number and type of decorations related to the venue size, while the number and types of giveaway related to the guest list and seating chart.

A member of the project support team was assigned the key to cupboard, along with the responsibility to track items in and out using the same configuration item records. He was not to allow anyone into the storage room or to take anything out without written permission from the project board. Using this system, the team remained in control of the outputs. On the actual day, the venue was decked out to perfection, and every attendee walked away with the right promotional toys and giveaways.

Prepare the quality management strategy

Description:

A key success factor of any project is that it delivers what the user expects and finds acceptable. This will only happen if these expectations are both stated and agreed at the beginning of the project, together with the standards to be used and the means of assessing their achievement. The purpose of the quality management strategy is to ensure such agreements are captured and maintained.

What this means

Consideration: How will this project team manage quality?

The project management team needs to decide how they want to manage quality before they can start to manage it on this project. Each project will be different, not only because of the people involved, but the size and nature of the project. Some organizations will have strict quality management guidelines, while others may not have any. Additionally, partnership projects will need to investigate the best method for this project: theirs, ours, or a combination of the two?

Sample considerations:

- How will quality planning be conducted?
- How will quality be controlled? What quality standards need to be adhered to?
- How will quality be recorded, verified and reported, and how often?
- How will quality checks be conducted, and the results documented?
- How will products be tested and approved?
- How will quality assurance activities be conducted, and how often?
- How will quality management be delegated throughout the project management team?

Thinking about quality at the end of a project is usually too late. Many projects fail because most of the time and energy is spent in the production of products and waiting to see if they pass a test at the end. If at this point they don't pass, it's normally too late or there isn't enough budget to fix the problems.

For every project, it needs to be determined how the quality of the products will be proved. It will always depend on the type, size and nature of the products being produced. It will also depend on the degree to which quality needs to be proved. If regulatory bodies are insistent that certain tests are conducted and passed in order for the product to be "certified," then those will need to be included in the decision of how the products will be tested. If the user wants guarantees of safety, then safety checks will need to be included.

These tests will need to be planned and resourced. Objective testers will review and determine if the product(s) meet the desired criteria. Objectivity is key in testing for quality. If the creator of a product tests it, there will be reason to doubt the validity of the test. The very human temptation to pass your own work can sometimes override the goal of impartial judgment for a test. Robot arms and crash test dummies, however, have the disadvantage of not being able to pass personal judgments. When human resources are involved in testing, it is best to use people who are not involved or connected to the production, so they can remain objective. These additional resources are not normally cost-free for the project, so planning for their time and costs will need to be built into the project's plans and overall budget.

Illustration

Refrigerator door manufacturers use mechanized robot arms to open and shut refrigerator doors up to 1000 times in a row to prove that the suction around the door will still work properly.

Car manufacturers set up mock crash sites and use crash test dummies to prove their quality.

IT developers hold user acceptance testing sessions on new systems to prove that they are usable and intuitive for their target audiences.

Food manufacturers run taste tastes and trials to prove a new product's appealing taste and market interest.

For safety reasons, certified professionals are employed on construction projects. In order to prove the weight-bearing capacity of foundations, they use complex, specialized machinery to conduct dynamic load tests.

Children's toys manufacturers are required to comply with multiple international safety criteria for their toys, which are tested by certified testers – normally adults – to prove their safety.

Drugs manufacturers test their products in a number of different ways – with laboratory experiments, animal testing, and even human testing – before claiming their safety for the general public.

If none of these types of tests apply to your products, then how far will you go to prove their quality? What is your reputation worth?

Prepare the communication management strategy

Description:

The communication management strategy addresses both internal and external communications. It should contain details of how the project management team will send information to, and receive information from, the wider organization(s) involved with, or affected by, the project. In particular, where the project is part of a program, details

---

should be given on how information is to be fed to the program.

If a formal stakeholder engagement procedure is needed, this should also be documented as part of the communication management strategy and should record the types of stakeholder, desired relationships and key messages, strategies for communication, and methods for evaluating the success of communications.

What this means

Consideration: How will communication both within the project management team and with other stakeholders be managed?

The project management team needs to decide how they want to manage communications before they can start to manage it on this project. Each project will be different, not only because of the people involved, but the size and nature of it. Some organizations will have strict communication management guidelines, while others may not have any. Additionally, partnership projects will need to investigate the best method for this project: theirs, ours, or a combination of the two?

Sample considerations:

- What communication methods will be used, and how?
- What communication tools will be used, and how? (For example, newsletters, e-mail, site visits, road shows, podcasts, etc.)
- How will communication records be kept and referenced?

- How will feedback from stakeholders be captured and managed?
- How will communication be reported, and how often?
- How will communication management be delegated throughout the project management team?
- How will stakeholders be analyzed?
- How will this project interface with program communication management requirements?

Illustration

Judy's program management team had already devised a fairly extensive communication management strategy. She was to follow the guidelines defined, as they were pertinent to her project. Due to the delicate nature and importance of her project to the program, sensitive and considerate communication was required. The program management team had, therefore, decided that all communication activities with external stakeholders would be conducted by them. No one on the project management team was allowed to discuss this project or their efforts with anyone outside the project management team. If questioned, team members were to instruct the requester to contact the program manager directly for information. In this way, Judy's project communication management strategy reflected the defined conventions and, at the same time, put procedures and mechanisms in place for dealing with highly confidential information within the project management team.

Set up the project controls

Description:

The level of control required by the project board after initiation needs to be agreed and the mechanism for such controls needs to be established – as does the level of control required by the project manager of the work to be undertaken by team managers.

Project controls enable the project to be managed in an effective manner that is consistent with the scale, risks, complexity and importance of the project. Effective project controls are a prerequisite for managing by exception.

What this means

Now that you've decided how to do things during this project, make sure the mechanisms you've decided to use are in place and ready for use. For example, if you wanted to use a Microsoft® Excel® spreadsheet to capture issues and changes, you would need to make sure that the spreadsheet template was created and stored in the correct location, and appropriate access permissions were granted for those who would need to access it. Also, if decisions have been made on how to delegate responsibilities for risk, configuration, quality and communication management throughout the project management team, then all the team members' role descriptions will need to be updated to reflect these decisions and new or amended authority levels.

Illustration

In his communication management strategy, Darren decided that he would set up a project e-mail address. This way, if any stakeholder – internal or external – needed to reach the project management team, they could use this designated address. He even came up with a clever address: *project_help@project.com.* This was his answer to capturing feedback and allowing the project communications to be truly bidirectional. Not only would it be a great communication tool to push messages out to stakeholders and team members about the project, but it would also act as a receptacle for collecting feedback.

The project board was so impressed by Darren's forward-thinking and proactive approach to engaging stakeholders that they failed to see that he had forgotten to actually create the account. The e-mail address was published repeatedly in project documentation, pamphlets, user guides and Internet and intranet sites. Yet whenever anyone attempted to use it, their messages were bounced back to them as "undeliverable." This did not sit well with the stakeholders, who felt that the project team was purposefully and maliciously trying to ignore their feedback by publicizing an e-mail address that didn't work!

The project board – who is responsible for the communications between the project management team and stakeholders external to that team – went into overdrive to repair relations. Measures were put in place to make sure this did not happen again. Not only was it logged in both the issue register and lesson log, but an immediate lessons report was distributed to the rest of the organization detailing this significant mistake.

Create the project plan

Description:

Before committing to major expenditure on the project, the timescale and resource requirements must be established. This information is held in the project plan and is needed, so that the business case can be refined and the project board can control the project.

Planning is not an activity that the project manager performs in isolation but, rather, something that should be done with close involvement of the user(s) and supplier(s). It is often useful holding planning workshops to help identify all the products required, their details, and the dependencies between them.

What this means

Even though the plan will change, an estimate is needed to establish an overall sense of what time, money and resources will be required for the project. A high-level, overarching estimate will suffice in giving the project board a mental picture of how long this project will take, as well as how much money and how many resources will be used and when. Without this picture, the project board may have the false impression that the project will take a lot less time, and so may begin overbooking resources and over-promising results. Or (possibly worse), they may assume the project will take a lot longer and start shying away from such a taxing investment of time, money and people. The project plan will be broken into stages, demonstrating the logical steps to get to the end result. The project board will be able to see the overall path, but will only need to commit to one stage at a time. After each stage, the project plan will be updated to show the latest thinking and the latest estimates on what it will take to complete the project.

Illustration

When the new local government officials were elected into office, they had made some fairly lofty promises. Their main pledge – and the one that won them the election – was to upgrade and improve all the local schools to the best possible standards within the next five years.

The timeline was clear: five years. The objectives were clear: to improve and update all the local schools. The details of how this was to be done, however, were not. A project plan only needs to show the major, high-level products and activities of the project, so that the overall timeline, costs and achievability of the end goal(s) can be assessed.

From their first day in office, the new officials were working on the new project. They couldn't complete it all at once, so broke the effort into stages. The School Upgrade Project (SUP) was launched to research, design, build, test, and rollout the new and/or improved schools to their community members, staff and students. The project plan showed a high level of the order of products (upgraded schools) and activities (designing, building and testing), but not the detail needed to actually achieve them. Additionally, it proved that the project could be done within the existing constraints of time, cost and quality, and provided an estimate for the timescale and resource requirements.

In order to complete the project plan, the project manager worked with community groups, students and staff members (the users), as well as architects, building contractors and building regulators (the suppliers). He facilitated multiple workshops and planning meetings to identify all the products and their dependency relationships.

In the end, it took a sixth year to complete the last few schools. Though their timelines were adjusted to address economic ups and downs along the way, they kept their promise and were consequently re-elected into office (another benefit for them).

Refine the business case

Description:

The outline business case produced during Starting up a Project needs to be updated to reflect the estimated time and costs, as determined by the project plan, and the aggregated risks from the updated risk register.

The detailed business case will be used by the project board to authorize the project and provides the basis of the ongoing check that the project remains viable.

What this means

Towards the end of the initiation stage, a lot more will be known about a project than could have been known in the Starting up a Project process. At this point, details about the project – which can be backed up with research and investigation – can be added to the business case. Timescales and costs can be verified through the project plan. Benefits can be validated via the benefits review plan, and an overall risk profile can be substantiated in the risk register. If, after the detailed exploration and analysis performed in the Initiating a Project process, a convincing and compelling business case can still be produced, then the project has a good chance of continuing on into the delivery stages, where the specialist work can finally begin.

Illustration

Dina owned the business case for the project. She was the project board executive. However, she did not have sufficient time or availability to actually produce the business case. She delegated this task to the Meghan, the project manager. Meghan was unfamiliar with the user community and their needs, their potential for change and their capacity to achieve benefits, so she relied on the senior user to help her identify and define the benefits for the project. Unfortunately, the senior user – in her enthusiasm, or over-enthusiasm – started to bite off more than she could chew. The benefits she was specifying were lofty at best, unrealistic at worst. With Dina (the executive) too busy to notice, no one checked or double-checked the validity of these benefits. The business case – the justification for doing the project – was over-reliant on shaky, somewhat questionable benefits.

As could have been expected, the project was completed on time and to budget, but did not deliver on over half of the predicted benefits. Lessons were learned – especially by the executive – to dedicate time and effort to assuring that the responsibilities to check and double-check the validity of the benefits being predicted are taken either personally or by a dedicated resource. For the executive – as the owner of the overall set of benefits from the project – this was a costly lesson, and one that she would not repeat again.

Assemble the project initiation documentation

Description:

There needs to be a focal point at which all information relating the "what, why, who, how, where, when and how much" of the project is:

- *Gathered for agreement by the key stakeholders*
- *Available for guidance and information for those involved in the project.*

This information is collated into the project initiation documentation. The project initiation documentation is an aggregation of many of the management products created during initiation and used to gain authorization for the project to proceed. It is not necessarily (and rarely) a single document, but a collection of documents.

What this means

This step does not state that a PID must be created, written or documented precisely, because it has already been created, written and documented. The PID has already been completed, refined and built up throughout the Starting up a Project and Initiating a Project processes. At this point, it merely needs to be converted into a format that is usable by the project's board members. The format of the documentation – as an e-mail, zipped, posted on an intranet site, or printed for a direct handover – will dictate how the assembly work will be conducted.

Illustration

Georgina – the senior supplier – is visually impaired, so required the PID to be printed in large print and presented to her in a binder. Maxine – the executive – is blind, so required the PID to be printed in Braille in several bound volumes. Celina – the senior user – is also blind, but preferred her copy to be sent electronically and without any graphics, so that her screen reader software, JAWS®, could translate it to her out-loud. The plan for the initiation stage detailed the tasks and resources required to compile the PID to these specifications for the project board members. The project manager followed this plan to ensure the right copy in the right format was delivered to the right member.

CHAPTER 8: CONTROLLING A STAGE

Work packages: Authorize a work package

Description:

It would be chaotic to have the people who are working on the project starting activities whenever they think fit. There must be a level of autonomy with the project team(s), but there will be wider issues involved of which they cannot be expected to be aware. It is therefore important that work only commences and continues with the consent of the project manager. The vehicle for this is the production, execution and delivery of a work package.

What this means

In order for a project manager to remain in control of a stage, s/he must know what is happening in that stage at all times. Through the use of work packages, s/he gets to decide how and when to authorize work to begin, continue and end. It's not enough for the project manager to delegate work to team managers; a corresponding acceptance of the work package will also be required. In the negotiations of asking for work to be completed and the accepting of that work, the project manager and team manager will need to decide and agree on procedures, communications, planning efforts, quality activities, targets, tolerances and completion procedures. Hopefully, a lot – if not all – of this will have been discussed during the planning process for the stage, where the team manager's involvement will have provided useful information and insight into the work being asked for in the work package.

Illustration

Cheryl sent an e-mail to Anne. Her e-mail asked Anne to pull together some facts and figures Cheryl needed for a report she was writing. She was going to be working on the report remotely, and would be in the office on Thursday afternoon to pick up the data. After sending the e-mail, Cheryl crossed this task off her list and continued working on her report. She took the train into the office on Thursday around noon, arriving just after one o'clock. When she got to the office, Anne was not at her desk. She looked around the office for Anne, and finally found her in the break-out area, chatting to some coworkers. The first thing she noticed was that Anne appeared very relaxed.

Anne confirmed Cheryl's fears: she had just gotten back from her holiday abroad late last night. She was really groggy today and was still working her way through the 300 e-mails waiting in her inbox.

Oops! Cheryl had forgotten the most important part of authorizing a work package: the all-important obligatory response from the team manager, indicating their acceptance. Without this, the project manager does not know if the team manager has truly understood or, in this case, even received the work package. If the team manager hasn't accepted it, there is little to no hope that the work will be done at all, much less to the standards and constraints defined in the work package. In the future, Cheryl will now request an e-mail or phone call acknowledging receipt of such e-mails.

Work packages: Review work package status

Description:
This activity provides the means for a regular assessment of the status of the work package(s). The frequency and formality of this activity will usually be aligned with the frequency of reporting defined in the work package(s) and supported by the stage plan for the current stage.

What this means

During the execution of the work package, the team manager will report information regularly via checkpoint reports. It is the responsibility of the project manager to review these reports against what was hoped would happen (as set out either in the agreed work package or the team plan). The actual progress information will need to be added to the stage plan and checked against the quality register in order to assess if progress is being made at the desired speed and accuracy.

Illustration

Jacqueline currently has 10 team managers working on 10 different pieces of work for her project. Today is Friday, so she is expecting 10 checkpoint reports via e-mail by the end of the day. Although her own highlight report is not due to the project board members until the end of the month, she has taken the decision to receive weekly reports from all the team managers. With 10 different streams of work occurring at the same time, she needs to be able to stay on top of the work and spot any problem or weak areas in order to deal with them before they become real issues.

When she receives the progress information from her team managers, Jacqueline refers to her supporting documentation to see if there are any new or potential problems. She reviews the work package and/or team plan to determine if the progress made to date is equal to that which was predicted, and if the work is still expected to be completed on time and to budget. Additionally, she reviews the quality register and configuration item records to ensure consistency of information between progress made to date and the quality management activities to date.

Based on all of this information from all 10 of her team managers, Jacqueline will need to update her stage plan to reflect this current data and any new forecasts or adjustments. She may need to update the risk register and/or issue register, as well.

Work packages: Receive completed work packages

Description:

Where work has been allocated to individuals or teams, there should be a matching confirmation that the work has been completed and approved.

Once approved, any subsequent changes to the product(s) must pass through change control. This should be an automatic part of any configuration management method being used.

What this means

Just because a team manager claims to be finished with a piece of work does not necessarily mean they really are. The project manager must look to the quality register to confirm that the products allocated to the team manager have been tested and approved. Only after confirmation that the work has been completed can the project manager release the team manager from their obligations regarding this work package. If the two parties should meet again during this project, it will be because of a new and different work package, because – as it has been confirmed – this one has been completed.

Illustration

John was very busy when the team manager phoned up to tell him that the product he'd been working on had been completed. John asked him if it had been tested. The team manager confirmed it had. John then agreed to take the product back and officially signed off on the work.

What John didn't know – and the team manager had forgotten – was that, although the product had been tested, there were a few minor errors that still needed correcting. The action items recorded in the quality check had been written on a scrap piece of paper that had become mixed up with and lost inside a large pile of other company documentation. This was then filed in a massive filing cabinet at head quarters three weeks later, never to be seen again.

When users started calling John to report problems with the product, John called the team manager. The team manager listened intently to what John was telling him about the problems and even agreed to help fix them, for a price!

The fact that John had signed off the product without checking the quality register to confirm the product had indeed been approved, meant that John now needed to re-hire the team manager to come back and fix the work. Realizing that this might strain the relationship, the team manager agreed to do the work at a discounted rate, but still needed to charge the project, as this was a commercial agreement and the project manager was authorizing a new work package. The old one had been officially and unequivocally received back.

Monitoring and reporting: Review stage status

> ### Description:
>
> *If the project is not checked on a timely basis, there is a danger that it will get out of control. There needs to be a balance between planning ahead and reacting to events.*
>
> *In order to make informed decisions and exercise rational control, it is necessary to compare what has actually happened with what was expected to happen and what might happen next (including issues and risks). It is therefore essential to have a steady flow of information that provides an overall view of progress and simple, robust monitoring systems to supply that information.*
>
> *The objective of this activity, therefore, is to maintain an accurate and current picture of progress on the work being carried out and the status of resources. This activity occurs at a frequency defined in the stage plan, may be triggered by project board advice, or forms part of the analysis of new issues and risks.*

What this means

In order for a project manager to fully understand how the stage that s/he is responsible for is performing, s/he needs information. It is not just the having of information though; the information will need to be checked and analyzed. In order for that information to be analyzed, it needs to be collected. In order for it to be collected, a method of collection needs to be planned for.

The stage plan will set out regular activities for the project manager (possibly with the aid of project support) to pull together data about the stage. Data will need to be amassed from the checkpoint reports received from the team manager(s), new and amended issues and changes in the issue register, new and amended threats and opportunities in the risk register, and updated records in the quality register. All of the data will need to be collated, reviewed and scrutinized against the planned estimates. If, based on the inspection, the stage is predicted to stay within its tolerances, then the next step will be to send a highlight report at the designated frequency required by the project board. If, however, the assessment predicts that the stage cannot be completed within its tolerances, then the next step will be to issue an exception report immediately.

Illustration

With the help of project support, Jayne set up arrangements to directly receive all the checkpoint reports from the team managers. Having gained these, she would then transfer the relevant data from the reports to the stage plan, issue register and risk register. Project support staff were also to be the first ones to be notified when a product had been completed, tested and approved, so that they could update the configuration item records to keep them inline with the updated quality register. Then, as project manager, Jayne would review the updated documentation every Tuesday to evaluate the stage status. This review often prompted her to perform one or more actions – such as taking corrective action or authorizing a new work package – or triggered her to move into the Managing a Stage Boundary process, if she was approaching the end of the stage.

Monitoring and reporting: Report highlights

Description:
The project manager must provide the project board with summary information about the status of the stage and project and distribute other information to stakeholders at a frequency documented in the communication management strategy.

What this means

During the project, the project board will be busy in management meetings and other senior management activities. They will have set the stage boundaries and delegated stage-level tolerances to the project manager. They know that, at the end of this stage, they will be notified of the stage's completion and provided with a plan for the next stage. However, it may be a long time before the current stage ends, and they will need confirmation and a reaffirming message from the project manager to tell them the stage is on track. A regular report (a highlight report) providing highlights of the work completed so far, the work to be done, and an update on issues, risks and quality will help the project board stay connected with the project, its status, and the justification for its continuation. Without this regular flow of information, the project board may feel disconnected and become dispassionate. The project will just fall off their radar. Highlight reports confirm to the project board that the project is being managed carefully and skillfully by the project manager. They may also prompt one or more members of the project board to make use of the "give ad hoc direction" activity, or ask questions or for clarification about the report. This will demonstrate their level of interest and involvement in the project effort.

Illustration

Gillian was asked by the project board to use a corporate template to report the project highlights once a month. In order to capture the right information for the template, she modified it for her team managers to use for their checkpoint reports. Now, she was guaranteed to receive regular, consistent progress information updates that she could easily summarize and present to the project board in whichever format they requested.

Issues: Capture and examine issues and risks

Description:

In the course of managing the project, various issues will occur and risks may be identified. They will arrive in an ad hoc manner and will need to be captured in a consistent and reliable way. Any member of the project, corporate or

> **program management, or other stakeholders may raise an issue or risk.**
>
> **Before making a decision on a course of action, each issue or risk should be registered and then assessed for its impact.**

What this means

As a PRINCE2® practitioner – one who uses and practices PRINCE2® – the project manager should know that the difference between a risk and an issue concerns the level of certainty surrounding it. A risk is a future uncertain event or set of events that may or may not happen, whereas an issue is a certain event that has occurred or will happen. Stakeholders in and around the project team may or may not also know this distinction. Many might be under the common false impression that risks are always in the future and issues are always in the past. So when these stakeholders with different interpretations call on the project manager with a problem, issue, concern, query, threat or opportunity, they may or may not be using the correct terminology to describe what they mean. Regardless of their use of these terms, the project manager needs a mechanism for capturing these comments and analyzing them with a consistent approach.

There are different procedures for both. The risk management procedures are documented in the risk management strategy and the change and issues procedures are documented in the configuration management strategy. The project manager will use the project's risk register and issue register to manage risks and issues as they are raised. The guidance in the strategies will help the project manager to assess the risks and issues correctly and either manage them within his/her limits or escalate appropriately.

Illustration

Matt created a database for the project. It was set up to capture both issues and risks. He web-enabled the database, so that anyone could log on and add new issues and risks from anywhere around the world. Because an issue or risk would already have been captured, he could then start from the point of examining and finish the processes from there. This freed up more time for him to spend managing the project, instead of doing administrative work. He decided that, weekly, he would review the database and perform issue and risk management activities. On paper, this looked like an efficient use of Matt's time and expertise. His project board agreed and authorized his plans.

After one week, Matt realized that the open access policy for the database was not working. Members of the public, hackers, and other miscreants were clogging up his database with useless rubbish. He reset the access limitations so only project management team members and identified project stakeholders could log on.

After two weeks, Matt realized that no one, besides himself, knew the difference between a risk and an issue. He reset the fields to capture the comments, and he then made the necessary distinction himself when managing them.

After three weeks, Matt realized that the peaks and troughs of the project activity were frequent and sporadic, making his once-a-week rule inadequate for managing the risks and issues. He increased his frequency to twice a week.

After four weeks, Matt found that he had struck the right balance for capturing issues and risks for his project. He updated his lessons log and reported on his findings in his next highlight report.

Issues: Escalate issues and risks

Description:

A stage should not exceed the tolerances agreed with the project board. The project manager can only take corrective action or maintain the status quo as long as the stage (or project) is forecast to be completed within the tolerances set by the project board. This activity applies where any corrective action with the project manager's control would not save the stage (or project) from going beyond the tolerances agreed. This applies to all types of issue and risk (or aggregation of them) that cannot be resolved within the tolerances set by the project board.

As it may take some time to gather the information to create an exception report, it is recommend that the project board be alerted as early as possible. Therefore, the project manager may wish to execute this activity in two steps: an early notification to the project board of the forecast exception situation in order to prepare them, followed by supporting information in the form of an exception report.

Escalating issues and risks is good practice and should not be seen as failure. The earlier that issues are escalated, the more time is available to implement any corrective actions.

What this means

If a new risk or issue impacts the stage such that its forecast now exceeds its tolerances, and there is nothing that the project manager can do to bring the stage-level tolerances back within their limits, the project manager no longer has the authority to make decisions regarding this stage. An exception report must be escalated immediately to the project board. There is no grey area around this distinction between forecasting inside stage-level tolerances and outside them. As soon as the project manager recognizes that s/he cannot keep the forecast for the stage within its tolerances, s/he must escalate the situation. Attempting to hide or mask the problem will only make things worse. The sooner the project board members, with their authority and levels of seniority, are involved with exception situations, the faster they can help resolve them. The project board will approve how this should work via the controls originally set up in the Initiating a Project process – i.e. if they want verbal exception reports in person or on the phone or, if they want written ones, what format they are required in, etc. Additionally, if the exception situation pushes the project outside the project-level tolerances within which they operate, the project board will need to escalate it to the corporate or program management above them.

Illustration

Joleen's team manager raised an issue about a local flooding, which was causing a time delay for his work package. After assessing the issue and looking at her options, Joleen decided to make additional time tolerance available to the team manager. When a second delay occurred due to the effects of a strike in Eastern Europe, she used her cost tolerance to pay for additional resources to help catch up on lost time. By the third delay – this time resulting from an active volcano in Iceland – Joleen was out of time and cost stage-level tolerances. She looked at the product descriptions to determine if there were any quality tolerances that could be applied, which could potentially lessen the workload for the team manager to counteract the delay. There were none. None of the options she considered would bring all the stage-level tolerances inside their limits. She then immediately escalated the issue via an exception report to the project board. She included all the options to resolve the situation that she could think of, but was not able to authorize these herself. She indicated that her recommended option would be to increase the stage's time tolerances, allowing Joleen to finish the stage within the new limits.

Issues: Take corrective action

Description:

Changes and adjustments to the project need to be made in a considered and rational way, even when they appear to be easily manageable and within tolerances.

In taking corrective action, the objective is to select and, within the limits of the stage and project tolerances, implement actions that will resolve deviations from the plan. Corrective action is triggered during the review of the stage status and typically involves dealing with advice and guidance received from the project board, and with issues raised by team managers.

What this means

If a new risk or issue does not cause the stage to exceed its tolerances, or the project manager is able to keep all the stage-level tolerances within their limits, then s/he has the authority to make decisions regarding the desired solution. The litmus test is that all the stage-level tolerances remain within their set limits as directed by the project board. If this can be done, then the project manager can get on with the stage and summarize the incident(s) and their resolutions in the next scheduled highlight report.

Illustration

Marguerite bought her sons a Scalextric toy car racing track. Her eldest son worked out, over a short period of trial and error experimentation, how to best maneuver around the tight corners and steep hills at just the right speeds and level of control in order to make it all the way around. The younger son kept losing control of his cars. He'd push them to go faster and faster until he lost control, spun off the track and was unable to complete the race.

The parallels to her work life were endless. The more work Marguerite tried to push through at breakneck speeds, the more problems and exceptions she ran into. Her boss was initially impressed with the speed Marguerite agreed to get things done. However, after the fifth exception situation in less than three weeks, he was becoming less and less impressed with her abilities. Marguerite reflected on this and decided to learn from her eldest son. By starting with a realistic plan then, over time, learning how to finesse the system and maneuver around obstacles, she would be able to stay in control – taking corrective action as she went, instead of escalating exceptions.

CHAPTER 9: MANAGING PRODUCT DELIVERY

Accept a work package

Description:
The fundamental principle is that before a work package is allocated to a team, there should be agreement between the project manager and the team manager as to what is to be delivered, the reporting requirements, what constraints apply, any procedures to be applied, and whether the requirements of the work package are reasonable and can be achieved.

What this means

This step figuratively or literally represents a handshake between the team manager and the project manager. The two parties must understand and agree to the work being requested and all the conditions of time, cost, quality, scope and effort.

The project manager is responsible for managing the project, not for doing the work. Therefore, s/he decides when work should be done, by whom and under what constraints. The team manager is paid to get the specialist work completed. When the project manager authorizes a work package, the team manager agrees (most likely after some negotiation) to do the work within the specified timeframe and under the agreed constraints.

The project initiation documentation contains information about how the project is to be managed. In order to create the work package, the project manager pulls out the relevant information pertinent to the team manager and conveys these rules and constraints within the work package (for example, how risks are to be managed, how configuration management is to be conducted, how changes are to be captured, assessed and approved or rejected, and how quality is to be managed, monitored and controlled, etc.)

Illustration

George, the project manager, signed a contract with a supplier to perform a piece of work. The supplier company did not use PRINCE2® to manage this piece of work, but that did not matter to George. What mattered to him was that the supplier agreed to the terms and conditions of the work package (in this case, the contract). The supplier agreed to make sure that the work would get done according to the contractual terms and conditions and that, when finished with the work, they would return it to George – again, according to the instructions agreed in the contract.

George's company had well-established working practices around the office. When incidents occurred, there were procedures for dealing with them. When communications were required, there were protocols that were followed. The company's document management system helped everyone comply with the organization's configuration management and version control requirements. So, when George authorized internal work packages, he did not need to write and agree a formal contract, as he did with the external supplier. Instead, he relied on their well-known and well-documented internal working procedures. Most of his internal work packages were in the form e-mails. The team managers would then reply to the e-mail to indicate their acceptance.

Execute a work package

Description:

The work has to be executed and monitored to the requirements defined in the authorized work package.

While developing the products, the team manager should not exceed the work package tolerances agreed with the project manager. The team manager can only proceed with the work package or take corrective action while the work package is forecast to complete with the tolerances set by the project manager. As soon as work package tolerances are forecast to be exceeded, the team managers should raise an issue to the project manager who will decide upon a course of action.

What this means

Once the team manager has agreed to (and perhaps negotiated) the constraints laid out in the work package, s/he gets on with the work. If there are problems or issues, the team manager raises an issue, so the project manager can manage them or escalate them to someone who can. If there are questions or conflicts, the team manager raises an issue, so the project manager can find the right resources to answer or fix them. If there are risks, the team manager raises an issue, so the project manager can use risk management to mitigate against them. This leaves the team manager without distraction and without obstacles, so s/he can get on with the work and report progress, as agreed.

Illustration

Birthe was not only a specialist in her field, but a stay-at-home mum as well. She had agreed to take on a part-time effort covering a two-week work package for a project. She also agreed to complete the work according to recognized industry standards. The time she reserved for working on the project was between 8 pm and midnight, when her children were in bed. The terms of the work package did not stipulate that she had to work during certain hours – only that she worked four hours per day. She sent her daily checkpoint reports in at midnight, and was thus in compliance with her daily progress reporting requirements. As the expert, Birthe got on with her work, which was impeccable. She completed her work within the agreed work package tolerances, and all of her products passed their quality checks with flying colors.

Deliver a work package

Description:

Just as the work package was accepted from the project manager, notification of its completion must be returned to the project manager.

What this means

Figuratively or literally, this step represents the second handshake between the team manager and project manager. This time, the two are agreeing that the work that was delegated to the team manager in the work package is, in fact, complete. The project manager will definitely need to be notified; possibly, project assurance and project support will also need to be notified when the work is complete. How all of this is to be done is documented in the work package.

Illustration

Sammie finished the last of the 20 products delegated to him in the work package. The previous 19 were sent back to project support for safe storage immediately after they had completed their quality checks. This time, Sammie not only had to call project support to come and pick up the last approved product, but he had to reference the work package to find out how he was supposed to advise the project manager of its completion. The instructions lead him to phone a mobile number and leave a voicemail message. After that, he was then to send a back-up e-mail to the project manager, confirming the voicemail message had been left. In his e-mail, he had to carbon copy three other team managers, one project assurance member and the manager of the project support team. Finally, once the voicemail and the e-mail messages had been sent, Sammie was supposed to turn his work badge in to the front desk at reception and sign the consent form for his hypnotic-trance-memory-removal therapy sessions, before being chauffeured to his first session.

CHAPTER 10: MANAGING A STAGE BOUNDARY

Plan the next stage

Description:
The stage plan for the next management stage is produced near the end of the current stage. Closure activities should be planned as part of the stage plan for the final stage.
Planning is not an activity undertaken in isolation. The project manager will need to consult with the project board, project assurance, team managers and possibly other stakeholders in order to create a viable plan. The more people involved in planning the more robust the plan will be (so long as the right people are involved).

What this means

Unless they are clairvoyant and able to see into the future, no project manager can accurately predict the distant future. Issues, risks and changes all impact a project in an ad hoc fashion, causing need for adjustments, modifications and corrections to be made along the way. For this reason, the project is broken into stages, and only the next stage is planned in detail. The project manager (possibly with the aid of team managers, project support and guidance from project assurance) should be able to plan in detail for the next stage with some level of certainty. This planning activity, however, must only happen as close to the start of that stage as possible. If done too early, then too many variants will have changed before the stage arrives; if done too late, there will be gaps of unproductive down time in the project, wasting time and resources.

Illustration

Natasha had been working in the organization for three years. She was accustomed to the company culture, its seasonal variations and its cyclical patterns. As a project support member, efficient in planning tools and techniques, she helped project managers set up and plan their projects. Even though she had assisted previous project managers in producing lessons reports about planning, she was still often asked to review draft plans to spot common errors.

The most common oversight she noticed was over-scheduling resources during summer months and at the end of the year. Most employees at the company took their annual leave at these times. On top of this, those still working during these peak times were already over-subscribed with activities to sustain the business as usual environment. The second biggest mistake was not involving key corporate functions in the quality checking of products. The human resources (HR), finance and procurement teams were always impacted by business changes, but rarely consulted about or involved in them. And the third common major error in plans was to plan too far in advance.

The company had a history of being severely impacted by the slightest of economic changes. Stage plans that made predictions for more than three or four months in the future tended to hit exception situations. Beyond this three- to four-month planning horizon, estimates in a stage plan were more or less guesstimates or flat-out guesses. Due to her experience and influence, Natasha helped many project managers within the company avoid these important planning errors.

Update the project plan

Description:

The project board uses the project plan throughout the project to measure progress.

The project plan is updated to incorporate actual progress from the stage that is finishing, and to include forecast duration and costs from the exception or stage plan for the stage about to begin.

Details of any revised costs or end dates are used when updating the business case.

What this means

Once a stage has been completed, the actual information about that stage can be documented in the project plan. If the stage was originally predicted to take three months, but actually took three months and two weeks, then this actual information will have knock-on effects on the whole project plan. In the original project plan, that next stage would have been predicted to have already started. The project plan now has to be updated to reflect it starting two weeks later, which may cause the entire project to finish late.

Once the next stage plan has been created, the new estimates for it can be documented in the project plan. These new and better projections have just been made in the previous step. The likelihood is that these new estimates are quite different from the original ones represented in the project plan – this due to experience, new information and lessons learned from the previous stage. These adjustments and corrections will need to be added to the project plan to provide a better, more accurate view of the overall project.

Illustration

Yoshi's original project plan predicted that, over the two-year timeline, each stage would take exactly three months to complete. After the first delivery stage, he realized that three months was too ambitious. The first stage had completed within its stage time tolerance of an additional three weeks; however, the original project plan was now out of date. Yoshi used the "save as" function on his project plan file and created a second version. This one recorded the actual information from the first delivery stage and new estimates for upcoming stages. In order to help create better, more accurate estimates for the plan, Yoshi consulted again with project assurance and the team managers who were going to be responsible for the work. Having already experienced one delivery stage, all were able to better contribute. Their estimates were more accurate, they made fewer assumptions, and they were able to identify and analyze risks more thoroughly. The second version of the project plan comprised stages with lengths ranging from three to five months (these depending on the different natures of the work being planned for), and a new overall time line spanning two years and two months.

Update the business case

Description:

It is a PRINCE2® principle that projects have continued business justification.

The project board is ordinarily only authorized to continue while the project remains viable (that is the benefits will be realized within the cost, time, quality, scope and risk parameters set out in the currently agreed business case).

Projects, however, do not take place in a static environment. The environment external to the project changes, as do the nature and timing of the project's products. The business case needs to reflect these changes and must be reviewed and amended to keep it relevant to the project.

As the executive is responsible for the business case, the project manager should consult with the executive when reviewing and updating the business case in preparation for project board approval.

What this means

With changes to the project plan reflecting new and updated forecasts for the remainder of the project, the timescales and costs sections of the business case – at the very minimum – will need updating. Furthermore, the need for the project will need to be checked and scrutinized. If the driving force behind the project disappears or diminishes, then the justification for the project expenditure is bound to disappear or diminish. A true and accurate portrayal of the continued justification for the project needs to be reflected in the updated business case.

Illustration

The project board has elected to pay for the correction of an exception in the current stage by de-scoping the project. The money initially allocated to creating one of the project's products was diverted to fixing the exception situation. The project manager was requested to produce an exception plan for this option, as well as to update the project plan, update the business case and write an end-stage report.

The effect on the business case was that the costs of the project remained the same, but the expected benefits decreased. The product being de-scoped contributed to the benefit of increasing sales by 50%. Without this benefit, the business case looked less and less desirable. However, when the project manager updated the business case to reflect these changes, she noticed that although the benefits were less than originally predicted, they were still well within the benefits tolerance for the project.

Report stage end

Description:

The results of a stage should be reported back to the project board, so that progress is clearly visible to the project management team.

The project manager gives a view on the continuing ability of the project to meet the project plan and business case, and assess the overall risk situation.

This activity should happen as close as possible to the actual end of a stage.

What this means

As close to the end of the stage as possible, the project manager needs to take stock, sum everything up, and give an account to the project board. As the person who knows the ins and outs of the project the best, the project manager needs to do a review and recap the previous stage. The project board will have been receiving highlight reports periodically since the previous decision was made – during the Directing a Project process – to authorize a stage or exception plan. However, this latest report is not about the progress of one stage, but is rather an overall assessment of the stage and a view of the project's continuing viability. As a measure to ensure objectivity, the project assurance team will review the end-stage report. Based on this report and the next stage plan, the project board will decide to continue their investment in this project or prematurely close it down.

Illustration

Jeremy was working on a high-profile project in his company. Since he was using PRINCE2®, at the end of his current delivery stage he sent an end-stage report to the project board. In it, he declared that he was officially finishing the current stage and was ready to take on the next one.

He gave a recap of the history and performance of the current stage. He provided an executive summary of the current state of the updated business case, offering information on the benefits that had been achieved to date and an assessment of the benefits still expected. He confirmed that the project was still on target to achieve its objectives, and that the current stage was just now finishing within its agreed targets and tolerances. He summarized the quality work completed and the performance of the products. He analyzed the current stage progress and provided statistics to show he was working within his tolerances. He ran through the issues and risks he had faced and how he had dealt with them. He summed up the team's efforts and identified some lessons learned. He even explained how he intended to apply those lessons with reference to the next stage plan.

Before handing the end-stage report and the supporting documentation to the project board, Jeremy showed it to project assurance. Minor errors and grammatical mistakes were caught in this review. Jeremy then sent the amended versions to the project board. He asked them to approve his current work and authorize him to move on to the next stage.

Meanwhile, Marley, another project manager at the same company, attempted to cut corners in his end-stage report. Relying on his own memory of the progress made, the performance of his team, the quality work conducted and the lessons learned, Marley's account of the stage was misleading and inaccurate. Immediately, project assurance picked up on the mismatch between the supporting documentation, previous highlight reports and basic common sense. When called on it, Marley realized what he had done. His earnest attempt to save time and effort by cutting corners could have been disastrous, reflecting poorly on him and his team. With a new perspective and diligence to observing the standards and processes the organization had put in place with PRINCE2®, Marley reworked the end-stage report to the agreed level of quality required for his project.

Produce an exception plan

Description:

If a stage or the project is forecast to deviate beyond its agreed tolerances, it no longer has the approval of the project board.

Exception plans are requested by the project board in response to an exception report. Although an exception plan will be produced prior to the planned stage boundary, its approval by the project board marks a stage boundary for the revised stage.

What this means

When a project manager is alerted to an issue, the first action s/he needs to take is to capture it on the issue register. After assessing the issue and determining its impact on the current stage and project tolerances, s/he must look for options to correct it. If the issue is beyond the authority levels of the project manager – as documented in his/her stage-level tolerances – s/he must escalate the issue via an exception report. Based on the report, the project board can choose to fix the problem, close the project, or request an exception plan to show in detail how the situation could be resolved.

If the project board asks for an exception plan, then the project manager should then use the Managing a Stage Boundary process to create one. In the exception report, the project manager would have presented several options for handling the exception situation. Based on these recommendations, or possibly one that the project manager had not thought of, the project board will request that the project manager re-plan.

Just because the project board has asked the project manager to create the plan does not mean that the project manager is authorized to use it yet. Once produced, the project board will need both the new plan and other additional information – an updated project plan, updated business case and an end-stage report – to help determine if they should continue to invest in the project or prematurely close it down.

Illustration

Planning takes a long time and a lot of effort. It usually entails several rounds of workshops with team managers and project support, as well as reviews with project assurance. Only once a feasible and workable plan has been created and agreed can it be considered ready to present to the project board. So, when Tina started working on the exception plan before hearing back on the project board's decision about the exception report, she was wasting her own time, as well as that of many valuable company resources. It turned out that the project board had not made their decision for two days because they were hotly debating the merits of continuing on with the project against those of prematurely closing it down. In the end, it was decided to close it down. No longer was the project worthwhile for the organization. Tina was directed to move into the Closing a Project process to close it down prematurely.

Later, when the invoices started showing up at her manager's cost centre, Tina had a hard time explaining why she had been conducting workshops using company resources she was not authorized to use. She had hired expensive meeting rooms, spent money on coffee and lunches, and pulled staff members away from their business as usual jobs in order to work on a plan that, in the end, was not needed. The project manager should only produce an exception plan when requested to do so by the project board. As the project board represents the link between the project and other stakeholders – including corporate or program management, there may be other considerations to take into account while they make their decision about the future of the stage and/or project.

CHAPTER 11: CLOSING A PROJECT

Prepare planned closure

Description:

Before closure of the project can be recommended, the project manager must ensure that the expected results have all been achieved and delivered.

What this means

Before closing down and handing things over, the project manager has to confirm that everything that had been set out to be delivered by this project has been. The project plan needs to be updated with all the actual information presented against the plans to prove all the work agreed on for this project has been completed. Additionally, a report will prove that all the products from the project have been granted "approved" status. The report – known as a product status account – will demonstrate that the products have all been tested and approved to meet their agreed quality criteria. And finally, the project manager needs to prepare to disband the team and get ready to release the project resources acquired for this temporary effort (for example, office space, computers, infrastructure, e-mail addresses, websites/intranet sites, etc.)

Illustration

Jose knew the end was fast approaching. His team had been working together for last two years, but, before they could disband, Jose needed their help to finish off the last remaining tasks. The team managers helped by providing a timely and complete work package and quality information to aid Jose in updating the project plan with all the actual information from the final stage. Project support helped confirm that every single product from the project was indicated as "approved" on the product status account. Project assurance for the senior user worked with Jose to confirm that the acceptance criteria listed in the project product description had all been met. Once complete, Jose sought approval from the project board to give notice to their program management team above them that his team could soon be released.

Prepare premature closure

Description:

In some situations, the project board may have instructed the project manager to close the project prematurely. In such circumstances, the project manager must ensure that work in progress is not simply abandoned, but that the project salvages anything of value created to date and checks that any gaps left by the cancellation of the project are raised to corporate or program management.

What this means

Either at an end-stage assessment or via ad hoc direction, the project board can request a premature closure. The issue register will need to reflect this project board decision, as it is "a relevant event that has happened, that was not planned, and requires management action." The issue will need to record the resolution as the board's decision to prematurely close down the project, as well as the effects on the project.

Before closing it down prematurely, the project manager has to confirm that what was agreed to be delivered up to this point in the project has been. The project plan needs to be updated with actual information up to this point. Additionally, a product status account will prove the products created to date have been granted "approved" status, meaning they have been tested and approved to have met their agreed quality criteria. And finally, the project manager needs to prepare to disband the team and get ready for an early release of the project resources acquired to date (for example, office space, computers, infrastructure, e-mail addresses, websites/intranet sites, etc.)

Illustration

A local council ran out of funding halfway through a building project. The objective of the project was to temporarily move residents out of their current public housing arrangements, demolish their dwellings, and rebuild better, more modern ones in their place. The project funding dried up after the residents were re-housed, but before the demolition activities could commence. The project board had no money left for the project, so they prematurely closed it down.

Even though the project did not finish, there were still completed products from the project that needed to be accepted by the council. In this case, the empty housing estate needed to be accepted by the council. It was completed and tested, in that all the residents had been moved and the building had been cleared for demolition. Additionally, the project had already acquired the necessary planning permissions for the new buildings. If new funding was to be found later on, the council would have in their possession products that could be used straight away to complete the remainder of the project. If they don't recognize these as acceptable products, then their next project or change initiative will incur needless additional costs to perform work that has already been completed and tested.

Hand over products

Description:
The project's products must be passed on to an operational and maintenance environment prior to the project being closed. This may happen as a single release at the end of the project, or the project approach may include phased delivery where products are handed over in a number of releases.
It is not a project activity to undertake benefit reviews post-project, only to plan for such benefits reviews to occur.

What this means

The person or people who will soon be taking ownership of the products created from this project need to be given the products. They will also need information about the products (for example, configuration item records and details of open issues and open risks, along with their planned/suggested mitigating activities). The management over the products in the business as usual environment will want to know that the products are acceptable, and so will require evidence of acceptance records. The management will also need to know about any pending next steps for the products they are about to take ownership of (for example, ideas for future upgrades, predicted timings for impending modifications, etc.)

Additionally, the benefits review plan will need to be reviewed and updated with any actual benefits that have been measured and realized to date. The remaining benefit reviews will be planned for post-project, but will not be conducted by the project team. This benefits review plan needs to be handed over to the senior user(s) and executive. The senior user(s) will be held to account for the benefits realization after the project. Here, however, they will be working in their business as usual roles – rather than as project team members – as the team will soon be disbanding.

Illustration

When Ashley purchased his brand new house, he didn't expect the estate agent to just hand him the front door keys and walk away. He needed more than that. He wanted the floor plans showing where the gas and water mains were located. He wanted the deed proving his outright ownership and the exact measurements of his property lines. He wanted the paperwork describing his home owner association rules and guidelines. He wanted a copy of his insurance and mortgage agreements. He wanted the warrantees that accompanied all the new household appliances. He expected all these things and more, so that he could not only own his new house, but he could use it – live in it, decorate it, paint it, grow a garden around it and refurbish it, if needed.

Evaluate the project

Description:

Successful organizations learn from their experiences with projects. When evaluating the project, the objective is to assess how successful or unsuccessful the project has been. It may also be possible to improve the estimation for future projects by analysing the estimates and actual progress metrics for this project.

What this means

As all the documentation has been updated with the actuals from the final stage, the project manager, in consultation with the project management team, can look back and review how the experience of the project was for them. An objective assessment about targets, milestones, changes, risk management, performance and quality can be made. As well as this, valuable lessons from this experience need to be captured and shared. The end project report – informed by the management products created, updated and configuration-managed throughout the project – will provide the useful assessment of the project's end result compared with its original intentions depicted in the project initiation documentation. The lessons report – informed by the issue register, risk register and quality register – will summarize key learnings that will be useful for any future project within the organization.

Illustration

Emily and Richard returned from their holiday in Greece. Their goal was to visit at least three islands, as well as the mainland. They wanted to see the Acropolis and four or five museums or churches. Their tour operator had provided them with all the tickets they needed to accomplish their desired itinerary. So why did they not achieve all of this on their trip? A thorough review of the events helped them see the problems and learn some valuable lessons for their next European excursion.

Richard enjoyed touring around the city of Athens more than he had anticipated, and prolonged their stay there by one day. Their problems started when they realized their ferry tickets were only valid for the date they were booked. They had to purchase new ones to replace the old ones. When they reached their first island, the hotel had cancelled their reservation because they did not show up the night before, but their credit card had been charged in compliance with the hotel cancellation policy. The hotel had already booked their room to another guest and there were no more vacancies. In fact, there were no vacancies at any of the hotels on the island. Richard and Emily were then forced to purchase more ferry tickets to another nearby island to find accommodation for the night.

When the time came for them to move on and catch up with their original itinerary, they discovered that the ferries to this island were not as frequent as the others. No ferries were due into port for another three days, causing them to miss their scheduled appointments and hotel reservations. They had to divert all of their energy and holiday budget into getting back to Athens for their return flights, or risk losing those as well and paying even more penalty fares to get home on time.

From their lessons learned on this travel experience, their new family motto was changed from "live for the moment" to "pay that bit extra for flexible travel arrangements!"

Recommend project closure

Description:

Once the project manager has confirmed that the project can be closed, a closure recommendation should be raised with the project board.

What this means

The communication management strategy will specify the stakeholders who will need to be informed of the pending project closure. The project manager will draft a notification (the closure notification) that, if approved by the project board, will be sent to the identified stakeholders, alerting them to the fact that the project is closing. All of the project's registers and logs can then be closed down and archived for future audits. The project management team will remain in place until the project board makes their final decision to authorize project closure.

Illustration

Collin reviewed the project's communication management strategy to confirm who needed what information about the closing of his project. Based on the strategy, he drafted the following items: a press release for the media, formal notifications to the suppliers suspending their contracts, and an internal company newsletter article announcing the successful completion of the project. He forwarded these to the project board with the end project report. If they decided to authorize its closure, the project board could then send these announcements out accordingly.

CHAPTER 12: ADDITIONAL SUGGESTIONS AND PROCEDURES

Business Case theme: Relationships between outputs, outcomes and benefits

Description:
In PRINCE2®:   • *A project's output is any of the project's specialist products (whether tangible or intangible).*   • *An outcome is the result of the change derived from using the project's outputs.*   • *A benefit is the measurable improvement resulting from an outcome that is perceived as an advantage by one or more stakeholders.*

What this means

The project is responsible for creating products. These products are the outputs, which are handed over to the user community(ies) for use in business as usual. Just because the users have access to or knowledge of an output does not guarantee that they will actually use it. The outcome is the consequence of actually using the output. A change in behavior (i.e. the outcome) happens by using the new output, and becomes embedded in the organization when it is stable and considered the norm. The benefit(s) are the measurable improvements caused by this change in behavior and new way of working.

Illustration

Sarah's boss purchased licenses for Microsoft® Outlook® (the output). He wanted everyone on the team to start using Microsoft® Outlook® to keep track of appointments and schedules (a change in behavior, i.e. the outcome). The benefits he wanted were for the company to be greener – killing less trees – and to be friendly – with everyone being transparent with their activities and schedules. Sarah, however, had an unusual attachment to her paper diary. Her life-long obsession with hand-writing out her daily schedule and being able to physically cross off items when completed gave her enormous satisfaction. She had yet to come across an electronic gadget or system that gave her the same level of pleasure. She had tried Microsoft® Outlook® before at her previous company, and found she was not able to stick with it.

When the order came from the boss himself, she really did give it a good try. At first, she tried entering her schedule into both the system and her paper diary, but that ended up taking too much time away from her actual work. She then only added meetings into Microsoft® Outlook® because she could not be disturbed during meetings; other activities she felt didn't warrant such protection from interruptions. So, for a while, her colleagues were aware when she was in a meeting and was not to be disturbed, but they were not aware of how else she spent her time. Those activities still went in her paper diary. Eventually, even the meetings stopped being recorded in Microsoft® Outlook®. No one knew what Sarah was doing, except for her administrative assistant, who had to keep ordering paper diaries for her.

Because Sarah was not using Microsoft® Outlook®, her behavior did not change. She continued to be ultra-private and eco-unfriendly. As a senior manager not partaking in the behavioral change, she set a poor example to others in the organization, who also preferred to keep privately held schedules (possibly not for the same reasons as Sarah). Thus, their behavior did not change either.

A definite divide started growing within the company, with those who complied with the Microsoft® Outlook® diary rule on one side, and those that did not on the other. The outcasts who didn't use Microsoft® Outlook® were seen as secretive, manipulative and politically ruthless. Not only did they not want to save the world by contributing to a greener workplace, they were contributing to a conflict-ridden work environment. None of the benefits of using Microsoft® Outlook® were being realized; in fact, the opposite was occurring.

Organization theme: Stakeholder engagement

Description:

Stakeholder engagement is the process of identifying and communicating effectively with those people or groups who have an interest in or influence on the project's outcome. It is usually carried out at the program level. All projects need to have some level of some stakeholder engagement, particularly if not part of a program.

Parties external to the project management team can exert a powerful influence on a project. Effective communication with key stakeholders, both internal and external to the corporate organization, is essential to the project's success.

12: Additional Suggestions and Procedures

What this means

The one rule with stakeholders is that you can't ignore them. If people feel ignored, they tend to get angry, disenchanted and despondent. If they hadn't been ignored, they could have been a true champion and advocate for your change efforts, but, after feeling slighted, it is unlikely they will support you (at least not until a lot of reparations have been made).

The one truism about stakeholders – which is sometimes the bane of the project manager's existence – is that you cannot choose them. The project management team members are chosen based on their skill, interest and availability. Project stakeholders exist whether you want them to or not.

In order to engage with stakeholders, their needs and interests need to be understood and a strategy put in place to either encourage their ongoing support, redirect their opposition into support or, at the very least, minimize the destructive and disruptive powers of their opposition.

Illustration

A junior project manager working on his first ever project was responsible for implementing a new car park on derelict land inside a suburban neighborhood. He did a fantastic job organizing the external suppliers clearing the land, resurfacing the land, painting parking spaces with the maximum use of space, etc. The one thing he didn't do – and didn't even occur to him to do – was to engage with stakeholders.

Property owners in and around the neighborhood saw the building work going on, but did not understand what it was or how it would impact them. Members of the local neighborhood association started joining forces, riling public opinion against the new site. On the day the car park opened for business, there were the local residents standing in front of the entrance, linked arm in arm, not allowing anyone to park there.

If only the project manager had bothered to engage with these stakeholders sooner. Then, they would have understood that the money generated from the paid parking would be reinvested back into their neighborhood. The lot would be manned 24/7 by security guards, who would deal with any riffraff traipsing through their community streets. And finally, parking would be restricted to 7 am to 7 pm, so no additional traffic would congest their streets at unsociable of the night. All of their concerns could have been addressed. Instead, pictures of their protest were plastered all over the front covers of the local newspapers.

Quality theme: Quality review technique

Description:

A quality inspection is a systematic, structured assessment of a product conducted in a planned, documented and organized fashion. There are a variety of systematic inspection techniques, some being specific to certain industries or types of product. PRINCE2® accommodates the use of these techniques, but also provides a useful quality review technique, which complements the use of a PRINCE2® product description.

12: Additional Suggestions and Procedures

> **Four review team roles:**
>
> * **Chair** – responsible for the overall conduct of the review
> * **Presenter** – introduces the product for review, represents the producer(s) of the product and coordinates and tracks work after the review
> * **Reviewer** – reviews the product
> * **Administrator** – provides administrative support for the chair and records the results and actions

What this means

Step one: Review preparation

Preparation entails taking care of the administration side of the review, checking that the product is actually ready to be reviewed, and distributing copies of the product to all the designated reviewers. It is important to note that, in this first step, the quality reviewers will actually review the product against the quality criteria described in its product description. If the product matches the quality criteria, or is within the defined quality tolerances, then the second and third steps may be achieved quite quickly.

If there are minor errors, such as spelling mistakes or misused punctuation, these can be marked up or annotated on the copy and returned to the presenter. However, if there are questions, concerns or comments about the product matching its criteria, then the reviewers are required to capture these on a question list, which will form the basis for the agenda for the second step: the review meeting.

Step two: Review meeting

In the review meeting, conducted by the chair and minuted by the administrator, the reviewers will discuss the product with the product's presenter, who will attempt to answer questions and clarify concerns. Together, the reviewers will discuss and agree the review results: either "complete," "conditionally complete" or "incomplete." If possible, and if the person/group with approval authority is present, the product can be signed off in the meeting, there and then. Regardless of the result, the chair will close the review and inform interested parties.

Step three: Review follow-up

If agreed actions have been identified, then the presenter will need to coordinate them after the review meeting. Each action will require a follow-up – as agreed by the reviewers in the meeting – to ensure they have been completed. Once all the actions have been completed, the product can be signed off by the chair as "complete." The administrator can then provide the review outcome information to the appropriate parties and update the quality records.

Illustration

One: Review preparation from the presenter's perspective

The recommendation paper that Nancy was working on was finally complete, just in time for the quality inspection that was scheduled for that week. Sylvia, the chair, called that morning to check she was ready. Because Nancy was the only producer of the product, she was in a good position to be the presenter as well. Sylvia also confirmed that all 10 of the reviewers were all set and ready for the review. Nancy sent copies of her paper to the reviewers.

Two: Review meeting from the chair's perspective

Sylvia opened the meeting by thanking everyone for taking time out from their busy schedules to attend the meeting. Since most of the 10 reviewers came from different areas of the organization and did not know each other, Sylvia asked everyone to introduce themselves and explain how this recommendation paper impacted their business area. From previous experiences, Sylvia knew that facilitating a group of strangers through an in-depth discussion would be difficult without them first understanding each others' perspectives.

Next, Sylvia asked Nancy to give a brief introduction to the paper, its background and purpose. After this, the group went through a product walkthrough. Nancy did a brilliant job walking the group through page by page, addressing the questions raised on the consolidated question list. Sylvia had sent her the consolidated list prior to the meeting, so Nancy would be prepared. And she was! She answered all their questions, and any items that required further actions were agreed by the reviewers and captured by Lillian, the administrator.

A few themes arose from the questions and agreed actions, so Sylvia led a group discussion to raise any other global or major questions. Each of these was then reviewed and actioned, all of which were also captured by Lillian.

The meeting lasted two hours and ended with the group reviewing all the action items, along with their responsibilities. The review result was "conditionally complete." Once the agreed actions had been fulfilled, the recommendation paper would be considered "fit for purpose."

Three: Review meeting from the administrator perspective

After the review meeting, Lillian still had a lot of work to do. She ensured that Nancy had the list actions, so she could coordinate them, as agreed in the meeting. She followed up with the reviewers that had responsibilities to sign off individual actions – as agreed in the meeting – so that the quality records could be maintained accurately.

She let Sylvia know when all of the actions were complete, so, as chair, she could sign off that the recommendation paper was now complete. She then let Nancy know, so she could start the process of getting the product approved. Finally, before filing away all the quality records from the review, Lillian communicated the review outcome to the 10 business areas that required the update.

Plans theme: PRINCE2® approach to plans

Description:

The philosophy behind producing plans in PRINCE2® is that the products required are identified first, and only then are the activities, dependencies and resources required to deliver those products identified ... Each step (of the seven

---

steps) in the planning procedure may need to be revisited on completion of later steps.

1. Design the plan
2. Define and analyze the products
3. Identify activities and dependencies
4. Prepare estimates
5. Prepare the schedule
6. Analyze the risks
7. Document the plan.

What this means

Step one: Design the plan

Of the seven steps for planning, the first one only needs to be done once, as a prerequisite to the rest of the steps. Once the format, presentation, planning tool and estimating method have all been chosen, then the rest of the planning activities can commence and be repeated, as necessary.

Step two: Define and analyze the products

The first repeatable step of the planning process is to define and analyze products for the plan (*see Chapter 12, Plans theme: Product-based planning for more information*). This step ensures that the plan will be created with the intent of creating products, and that these products will be within the agreed scope of the plan.

Step three: Identify activities and dependencies

Once the products have been defined and analyzed, the project manager (possibly with the assistance of project support and team managers) will begin to identify the activities required to create the products. If an activity is identified that has nothing to do with the creation, modification, acquisition, confirmation or approval of the plan's products, then the activity should be re-examined to ensure that it is really needed for the plan. Project resources are usually quite expensive – if not in money, then in time and opportunity costs – and so doing an activity "just because" comes at a great expense to the project and the organization.

Step four: Prepare estimates

Based on the estimation method chosen in the planning prerequisite, time and cost estimations will need to be made for the activities. It is important to use the estimating method identified earlier. If it is successful for this plan, the lesson learned can be to repeat its use for future plans. If it is unsuccessful, it may need to be changed or modified accordingly for future plans.

Step five: Prepare the schedule

The product flow diagram from product-based planning will be an excellent starting point for preparing the schedule. It shows the logical order of the creation of the plan's products. However, a lot of new information will now be known about the activities required for the plan – for example their estimated durations and costs, and resources availability. Some, if not all, of the flow will be modified to fit within these constraints when preparing the schedule.

Step six: Analyze the risks

Running alongside steps two to five is the step to analyze the risks. This exists because of the frequent identification of risks during the planning process. At each step, more information will be known about the plan and, therefore, more information will be known about what can go wrong (or right) with it. For each risk identified, a new item will need to be added to the risk register, and the chosen mitigating activities will need to be added to the plan.

Step seven: Document the plan

Once the plan has gone through its iterative cycle enough times to ensure there are no more risks to be identified or managed and all the products and estimated activities have been scheduled, then the plan can be completed. A final written narrative can be added to describe the plan and the thinking that went into its creation (for example, explanations of the constraints, external dependencies, assumptions, monitoring and control requirements, and any risks mitigation activities).

Illustration

Elizabeth decided to bake her first ever cake from scratch. She decided to use pen and paper to keep track of all the different aspects of baking; since she was so new to it, she didn't think she could keep it all straight in her head. The estimation method she chose to use was to double the preparation times recommended in her cookbook, but use the exact baking times.

She started her planning by defining the products – in this case, the ingredients she needed. She noted if she had the products already (external products) or if she would need to buy new ones (internal products). External products are ones that are required for the project, but they either already exist or are being created by someone else, such as another project. Internal products are ones that this project is responsible for creating, obtaining or modifying. Once Elizabeth had understood all the ingredients required, she identified the activities. She determined that she would need to buy the ingredients, mix them, and bake. The dependencies for these activities were that they must be done in that order. She estimated each activity using her estimation method, then scheduled them, so that the cake would be ready in time for dessert that evening. She ensured all her resources (the pans, oven and cooling tray) were going to be ready and available at the times she needed them.

As she reviewed the schedule, she built in a few fall-back plans, in case things didn't go according to plan. If, by the time the cake was due to go in the oven, she was running more than 10 minutes late, she would call the bakery down the road and order a take-away dessert instead.

Finally, Elizabeth documented her plan. She consolidated all her notes and ideas into a clear, concise narrative, reminding herself of her own planning assumptions (that she would not be interrupted, for example), her monitoring and control requirements (the use of the kitchen timer bell set at key milestones, for example), and her key risks and their responses (if running late, she would order in, for example).

Plans theme: Product-based planning

Description:

PRINCE2® uses a technique known as product-based planning to identify, define and analyze the plan's products:
* *Write the project product description*
* *Create the product breakdown structure*
* *Write the product descriptions*
* *Create the product flow diagram.*

What this means

Step one: Write the project product description

Through discussions with the senior user and executive, the project manager must capture the customer's quality expectations and help them to define these in terms of measurable acceptance criteria. These measurable acceptance criteria will form the basis for the eventual sign-off and acceptance of the project at its completion. This description will only be required for the project plan. It may be updated at various points throughout the project – when requested by the project board via ad hoc direction – using the project's formal change control procedures.

Illustration: The project is to make a cheese sandwich for lunch. The expectations are that it is delicious, large enough to be satisfying, and fresh enough to be desirable. The measurable acceptance criteria include that it is made on the day it is served and has white bread and Swiss cheese (*to be continued*).

Step two: Create the product breakdown structure

Next, the project is broken down into its major products for the project plan. For stage and/or team plans, the major products may be broken down even further to suit the level of plan required. Breaking down a product means identifying two or more sub-products or component pieces that make up the product. This can be done continually until the minutest component has been identified. However, if not required – due to the size and nature of the project and/or the plan – then it is not recommended to go into more detail.

Illustration *(continued)*: The product breakdown structure should include the component parts of the cheese sandwich for lunch:

- Two slices of white bread
- Two slices of Swiss cheese
- Two slices of tomato
- One leaf of lettuce
- One pat of butter
- One pinch of salt
- External product: serving plate (external because another project is responsible for choosing the lunchtime tableware, and this project must use what they decide – it is external to our control).

(*to be continued*)

Step three: Write the product descriptions

Once a product has been identified as required for the plan, a product description for that product needs to be created. Many of the products will not be created during the first (few) stages. Neither the project manager nor the team manager will be able to remember the details of the product if they are not captured in a formal product description.

A good test to see if all the required products have been identified is to compare the project product description with the sum total of the product descriptions. They should be equal to each other, with nothing new added and nothing originally intended forgotten.

Illustration (*continued*): For each of the products identified, product descriptions should define their minimum quality criteria and any allowable tolerances. For example, is there any tolerance around the choice that the cheese must be Swiss cheese? Will English mature cheddar suffice? Do the two slices of white bread have to be of a particular kind? Can it be white focaccia flat bread? Or white pitta bread? (*to be continued*)

Step four: Create the product flow diagram

One final step of product-based planning involves identifying the logical order of creation for the plan's products. In a one-directional flow, the products are sequenced in the order in which they should be created. For example, a draft product must precede the final version. This allows the planners to identify areas of risks where dependencies exist, especially from external sources.

Illustration (*continued*): The flow diagram will help determine if there are any dependencies in the creation or production of the products. For this example, all the sandwich products can be created, obtained or modified in any order – even concurrently. When multiple products can be created concurrently, this may indicate that the project work can be divided amongst several team members, who can work on separate pieces/products at the same time. This valuable information will come in handy during the scheduling step of the planning process. Alternatively, if a project's products have very strict linear production dependencies – i.e. each product cannot be started until the previous one has been completed – then, regardless of the number of resources thrown at this project effort, it will have little impact on the speed to completion.

Risk theme: The risk management procedure

Description:

PRINCE2[®] *recommends a risk management procedure comprising of the following five steps:*
- *Identify (context and risks)*
- *Assess (i.e. estimate and evaluate)*
- *Plan*
- *Implement*
- *Communicate.*

What this means

Step one: Identify (context)

It is important to understand the project's objectives and its risk management strategy for dealing with risks threatening those objectives. This contextual information will help with understanding how and why certain risks warrant extreme risk responses, and why others do not.

Step two: Identify (risks)

After understanding the project's context, it is easier to start identifying the project's risk. These are initially captured in the daily log during the Starting up a Project process, and are then moved to the risk register from the Initiating a Project process onwards throughout the project. The best way to capture individual risks is to state them in a cause-event-effect arrangement. The cause of a risk is the known element, the event resulting from the cause is the uncertain element, and the effect summarizes the "so what?" element that indicates why this risk is even being considered for management.

Step three: Assess (estimate)

Every risk identified and captured in the risk register needs to be assessed by providing estimates for its impact, probability and proximity. The guidelines and scales for producing these estimates will be defined in the risk management strategy. Simple scales for impact and probability might offer "high," "medium" and "low" scores, with definitions or criteria for each. Proximity might be measured as "near-term," "mid-term" or "long-term," with explanations for each.

Step four: Assess (evaluate)

Having an understanding of how big one risk is to the project is important, but equally important is an understanding of what the overall risk profile of the project is. By adding up all the threats and opportunities identified, a useful summary of the project's risks can be established. This is important for the project board when they are making decisions about the project. If the project becomes too risky, they may wish to prematurely close it down.

Step five: Plan

After assessing the risk for its size of impact, probability and proximity, response activities need to be identified to manage the risk. Or, alternatively, a measured decision not to manage (and accept) the risk needs to be made and recorded for future reference. The response activity will need to be proportional to the probability and impact of the risk. The proactive actions will need to be included in the plans. Separate fall-back plans may need to be created and resourced for any reactionary activities chosen to mitigate the risk.

Step six: Implement

Once the risk response has been chosen and included in the plans, it is the responsibility of the risk owner to manage the risk and it's identified response activities. If the risk owner is too busy to actually fulfill these activities, s/he may delegate the tasks to a risk actionee.

Step seven: Communicate

Throughout the entire risk management procedure, there needs to be constant, bidirectional flow of communication. The project management team needs to feel secure and confident in raising risks without recourse from political powers, blame or punishment. Reporting on risks needs to be open and transparent throughout the project, at all levels.

Illustration

Every autumn, Manjit faces the same threat on her journey to work. Because there will be leaves falling on the train tracks (the cause), the trains may be late (the uncertain event), and Manjit may be late to work (the effect). She has already begun informally managing this risk by mentally noting this problem at the end of the summer (identify). She assesses the risk by looking at the probability, impact and proximity. Because the train operator has put up a poster in her train station this autumn, warning passengers of possible delays due to leaves on the tracks, Manjit decides that the probability is high this year. The impact of being late to work is also high; she has been late before and is already on a written warning for punctuality. The proximity is near-term and constant throughout the autumn.

Because this risk is a threat, Manjit has six options. To avoid the threat, she could choose an alternative mode of transportation to work, such as driving her car or riding her bike. That way, any train delays would not impact her journey to work. She could reduce the risk by getting up earlier and taking an earlier train. Even if the earlier train was to be delayed, chances are it wouldn't be so delayed that she would be late to work. She could get up at the normal time and attempt to take her normal train – hoping it wouldn't be delayed – but have a fall-back plan in place to take a taxi to work if it was. She would need to ensure she always had enough cash on her every morning, in case she needed to call a taxi. No taxi driver would take her to work for free. There is no way for Manjit to transfer or share this risk, as the train operator is not prepared to accept any responsibility for delays due to leaves. Their placement of the poster in the station communicates this unwillingness loud and clear. And finally, Manjit could accept it, choosing to do nothing about the risk and continue to monitor it. If only she wasn't on a written warning already, she might be tempted to accept it. However, she elects to trial the reduction option first and then use her fall-back plan only if needed. By taking this course of action, she has allocated ownership of this risk to herself (she is the risk owner) and retained responsibility for the actions (she is also the risk actionee).

Change theme: Configuration management procedure

Description:

Configuration management procedures can vary, but they typically comprise five core activities:

- *Planning*
- *Identification*
- *Control*

- **Status accounting**
- **Verification and audits.**

What this means

Step one: Planning

Decisions about how much configuration management is needed for a project are made when creating the configuration management strategy. For example, the decision may be to only identify and manage the configuration of major products for small, simple projects, especially those with no additional resources to fulfill the project support role. Alternatively, for a large, complicated project, tighter control on all the elements and component pieces may be required, leading to the identification and management of small, detailed products, including their different states and components.

Step two: Identification

Once the rules have been set and agreed for configuration management, then the rules must be followed. If the rules are to only identify and manage major products, then, in product-based planning, only major products are identified.

Step three: Control

A product that has been passed through to "approved" status has been created, tested and approved based on the quality criteria defined in its product description. The product is considered perfect: exactly the way the customer wants it and needs it. No changes should be made to an "approved" product, except through the project's formal change control procedures. Even then, the original "approved" product will be kept by the project and a copy released for changes to be made to. This way, if problems occur when making changes to the copy, the original will be safe and another copy can be reissued. All of these procedures will also be agreed and documented in the configuration management strategy.

Step four: Status accounting

To gain a true picture of the different product statuses, a report indicating the statuses can be pulled together. Parameters for the report can be set, so that only certain products are reported on (for example, all the products from a stage, all the products from a work package, etc.), or all the project's products are reported on.

Step five: Verification and audits

In order to feel confident in the accuracy of the status accounting report, a series of regular verification checks and audits is required. As project support staff are normally the ones maintaining the configuration item records that house the status information, someone else will be needed to conduct these checks and audits. The project assurance team would be an ideal candidate for this step, as they are often given the task of checking and reviewing management products.

Illustration

Ellen, a member of the project support team, was in charge of the project's configuration library. She spent most of her time updating the configuration item records with new information as she received it. Many of the project's specialist products were designed in the UK, developed in India, manufactured in China, and handed over to partner organizations in the USA. At any given point, Ellen's tracking and recording mechanisms were able to detect all of the products' statuses, locations, and current owners.

When the unions at the ports in California, USA went on strike, Ellen raised an issue regarding the fact that many of the project's major products were currently in transit, heading from China to California. One cargo ship had not yet left Chinese waters and was turning back, delaying the journey for when the industrial action had been resolved. The other two ships carrying the project's products were already halfway across the Pacific Ocean. They had to continue on and hope that the strike would be resolved when they reached American shores.

When they got close to their ports, the strike continued, so the ships were diverted. One ship was sent north to Canada, the other south to Mexico. The products sent to Canada were quickly tracked down, as Canadians speak English and use relatively similar systems to those at US ports. However, the products sent to Mexico took ages to recover. Above and beyond the language barriers, the Mexican systems and port protocols were significantly different. Configuration management helped Ellen track these items until they were eventually recovered.

Change theme: Issue and change control procedure

Description:
PRINCE2® *provides a common approach to dealing with requests for change, off-specifications and problems/concerns:*   • *Capture*   • *Examine*   • *Propose*   • *Decide*   • *Implement.*

What this means

Step one: Capture

Anyone can raise an issue. The exact procedure for how it should be done should be documented in the configuration management strategy under the "issues and change control procedures" section. However, not everyone involved or interested in the project will know, or even have access to, these documented procedures. Their first impulse should be to contact the project manager. The project manager will have documented the configuration management strategy and will, therefore, know its contents intimately. S/he can then take down the issue in the manner and format defined in the strategy. Because of the administrative nature of this task, the project manager may have delegated some or all of this step to project support.

Step two: Examine

Once captured, a full and proper examination of the issue must be conducted. The assessment should consider the impact of the issue on the achievement of the project's objectives, as well as the impact on the six areas of tolerance within the project manager's control: time, cost, quality, scope, benefits and risks. An assessment of the impact against the overall project tolerances should also be carried out.

Step three: Propose

The project manager should investigate several options for dealing with the issue, including the option to do nothing. If s/he has the authority to act over the issue, then the project manager can move on to the next step. If the issue pulls the project manager outside of his/her stage-level tolerances, then s/he must escalate the issue via an exception report first.

Step four: Decide

Once the issue or exception has reached the right level of management (the person or group who has authority to decide on the corrective action), he/she/they can make a decision about it. Their decision must be recorded and cross-referenced in the issue report and/or issue register. Any corrective action should be reflected in the appropriate plan(s).

Step five: Implement

Based on the decision made about the issue or exception, the project manager should implement the actions and include them in the plans. The results of these actions may also need to be updated in the issue report and/or issue register.

Illustration

A user called the IT office and reached an IT team member working on the new system that had just been rolled out into the user's department. The user requested that a certain field on the user interface screen be moved from the left hand side to the right. The team member saw it as a minor cosmetic request. He happened to have that file open at the time of the phone call, so he agreed there and then to change it for the user.

At around 3 am that night, as the new system was going through its normally scheduled batch processing, it started to fail. Because of the failure, senior managers around the country were receiving text messages to call into an emergency conference call. As it turned out, 13 related systems that were searching for information from the field which had moved were programmed to look for it in a certain location. When it was moved, they could no longer locate the information and were no longer able to communicate or continue with the batch processing. A lot of angry and tired managers on the conference call were demanding heads roll.

Never in a million years should the IT team member have taken such a change decision without following a formal change control process. Even if s/he had the authority to make decisions about requests for change, an assessment of the impact from that change would have immediately shown that it was not a cosmetic alteration, but rather an intricate and complicated modification.

The same concept applies to projects. When undetected, undocumented changes that occur on projects are no longer operating in a controlled environment. When users want to add seemingly minor additions, when suppliers want to remove seemingly duplicate products, and when new legislation requires seemingly small adjustments for compliance, the project manager's knee-jerk reaction should be to pull out the issue log and start capturing.

Progress theme: Controls

Description:
The project board controls: authorizations, progress updates and exceptions and changes. The project manager controls: authorizations, progress updates and exceptions and changes.

What this means

How does the project board retain accountability for a project that they do not have the time to actually execute themselves? They are in the position to divide the project into smaller portions, known as stages. They delegate a stage at a time to one individual, the project manager, who then agrees to complete the stage within given constraints (stage-level tolerances). Progress information is sent to the project board at regular intervals confirming agreed progress (highlight reports). If situations arise that pull the stage outside of the agreed constraints, there is a mechanism (exception reports) in place to bring the project board up to date with the situation in order to make an informed decision to correct it (or not).

Once in charge of a stage, the project manager does not actually do the work, either. Instead, s/he breaks the stage work into smaller portions – known as work packages – and delegates these to team managers to create the specialist products. The team managers send progress information at regular intervals to confirm their agreed progress (checkpoint reports). If situations arise that pull the work package outside of the agreed constraints (work-package-level tolerances), there is a mechanism (issue reports) in place to bring the project manager directly into the situation. The project manager can then, if necessary, capture, assess and escalate, or take corrective action if not.

Illustration

The art of controlling work without having to do the work is also known as the art of delegation. Delegation involves dividing work into jobs or responsibilities, asking others to do those jobs, monitoring their work, stepping in only if needed, and then agreeing when it's all complete. A "thank you" would also be a great idea.

Patricia's project board delegated the entire project to her, providing her with so many tolerances that, if she came across any issues, she was guaranteed to be able to handle them on her own, without bothering them. The board members were not that interested in the project, its progress or its results. Patricia asked for a pay rise. She was, in fact, being asked to perform both her job and theirs.

Patrick's project board delegated two-week stages and gave him zero stage-level tolerances. Patrick updated his CV and got out of there. His project board either consisted of maniacal micromanagers, didn't trust him as an effective project manager, or, worse, was unable and unwilling to delegate. Every issue Patrick would hit on his project would take him outside of his zero tolerances, forcing him to raise an exception report. The project board would be making every decision for the project – in effect, doing their jobs as well as Patrick's. In his case, Patrick wasn't needed.

Health check

Description:

PRINCE2® provides process-oriented checklists that can be used at various points in the project to assess that the key aspects of PRINCE2® are adequately addressed.

What this means

The health check offers a comprehensive question set that will help guide and inform an auditor or reviewer in finding strengths and weaknesses of a project. This tool can be used by project assurance when they want to perform a project review. Alternatively, the project manager may want to self-diagnose problem areas within his/her project. Even an outside expert wishing to conduct an official audit could use this tool. The starting point for the questions depends on how far the project has progressed through the process-based life cycle.

Illustration

Harry was hired in as project assurance for the executive to work on their biggest project to date. The executive was too busy to understand why she was feeling so nervous about the project. She knew she didn't have much time to deal with the project manager, and was accepting everything he said at face value; but something was just not right. Harry, who had had years of experience managing successful projects, decided to start with a full assessment of the current situation. He asked the executive where they were in the project – the beginning, middle or end. He also asked the project manager the same thing. When he got two different answers, he realized there was an obvious communication gap. He broke out his PRINCE2® manual, started with Appendix E: Health check, and began asking questions.

This tool pulled out several key areas where the project management team was falling down. It was not just the project manager, but several of the inherent corporate or program systems in place that were stopping the communication flows required for this large project. Without the health check, this project may have died a terrible death, taking personal and professional reputations down with it. As it was, Harry saved the day by using common sense and referring to best practice guidelines to find the problem.

CHAPTER 13: TAILORING PRINCE2®

Tailoring successfully

Description:

PRINCE2® can be used whatever the project scale, complexity, geography or culture, or whether it is part of a program or is being managed as a "stand-alone" project. Indeed, it is a principle that a PRINCE2® project tailors the method to suit such contexts.

Tailoring refers to the appropriate use of PRINCE2® on any given project, ensuring that there is the correct amount of planning, control, governance and use of the processes.

What this means

PRINCE2® is designed to be used with any project – big or small, simple or complex, part of a program or stand-alone, in a single organization or multi-organizational, an internal relationship or a commercial relationship, in the private sector or public sector, etc. No matter what the situation or arrangements for the project, considerations of how extensive and how formal PRINCE2® as a framework will be applied need to be made and understood by all interested parties. Without care, PRINCE2® can be become overly bureaucratic for smaller, simpler projects, or gain larger, more complex projects the reputation of being "PRINCE2® in name only" (PINO).

Illustration

Project: Small, simple, local

Helena had a 45-minute meeting with her boss (the executive) in a coffee shop to go over the basics of the project idea. When they were through, her boss authorized her to move into the Initiating a Project process. Helena documented the results of their discussion in a follow up e-mail. For this small, simple and local project, an informal discussion between the executive and project manager was sufficient to cover all the points of the Starting up a Project process.

Project: Large, complex, global

Horace's new project involved partnership organizations, including the central government. Never having worked on such a massive and formal project before, it took Horace a while to figure out how to manage it appropriately. Very formal control mechanisms were put into place to keep a tight hold on the all the facets of the project. With input from his own trial and error, advice from project assurance and lessons learned from previous large, organic projects, Horace developed a complete system with which he actually felt in control of the work instead of that the work was controlling him.

To start with, every project management team member signed an official role description in order to participate in the project. The original copy was held in the project's central files, another was given to the team members for their own reference, and a third was kept in their HR employee records file. This degree of formality ensured everyone completely understood their responsibilities in participating on the project team, as well as their authority limits and reporting lines within the project.

All management products, except for the exception report, were subjected to quality reviews with the project assurance staff members, before being sent to the project board. All management products sent to the project board were sent as hard copies and required two signatures – one for receipt and one for approval or rejection.

Configuration management for the project's products was to be controlled by the team of configuration librarians in the project support office ... and on and on the tight controls were put in place.

Horace became known as a well-organized and much admired mini dictator for the project, but he held that title in high regard. It was precisely because of these formalities that the large and often unwieldy project was kept in an efficient state throughout.

CHAPTER 14: ROLES

Project board

Description:

The project board is accountable to corporate or program management for the success of the project, and has the authority to direct the project within the remit set by corporate or program management as documented in the project mandate.

The project board is also responsible for the communications between the project management team and stakeholders external to that team (e.g. corporate and program management).

What this means

The project board members need to have enough authority within the organization to make decisions about the project (for example, to authorize plans, allocate resources and represent their specific area – business, user or supplier). The members must demonstrate decision-making skills, leadership and commitment throughout the project. Ideally, the members will stay in their roles throughout the project's life.

Illustration

Project: Small, simple, local

Joseph, the most senior manager of the department, took on the roles of executive, senior user and senior supplier for the project. He would also perform all the assurance activities for all three roles.

Project: Large, complex, global

Joanna, the most senior manager of the organization, took on the role of executive. She appointed three other senior managers to fulfill the senior user role, and two senior managers to fulfill the senior supplier role – one internal and one external. The six members of the project board met formally at end-stage assessments and informally and/or virtually on a quarterly basis. Project assurance functions for all three project board roles were delegated to individuals in the quality assurance department, as well as to the internal finance manager, who was to perform additional business assurance.

Executive

Description:

The executive is ultimately responsible for the project, supported by the senior user and senior supplier. The executive's role is to ensure that the project is focused throughout its life on achieving its objectives and delivering a product that will achieve the forecast benefits. The executive has to ensure that the project gives value for

---

> **money, ensure a cost-conscious approach to the project, balancing the demands of the business, user and supplier.**
>
> **Throughout the project, the executive is responsible for the business case.**
>
> **The project board is not a democracy controlled by votes. The executive is the ultimate decision maker and is supported in the decision making by the senior user and senior supplier.**

What this means

As the owner of the project, the executive takes on the most responsibility for the project. There can only be one executive on a project team. If there are two or more people fulfilling this role, there will be guaranteed confusion, misdirection and frustration. For true ownership to exist, only one person can assume accountability – one person whose neck is on the line. If the project was to go horribly wrong due to poor project management, it would not be the project manager who got blamed, but the executive (even in a no-blame environment). How could s/he have let the project go on and on without the requisite project management skills, resources and funding in place? If the project was to go horribly wrong due to other reasons (for example, economic, environmental, societal or technological changes) then there should be no one to blame. It would be up to the executive to either close the project prematurely or escalate the situation to corporate or program management.

Because the executive appoints the project board members, the board members are accountable to him/her. They may be peers of the executive in their line management jobs, but, on the project management team, they are supporting functions to aid the executive in decision-making for the best interests of the project. The executive will arrange the project funding and chair the project board meetings.

The executive has responsibility for the function of business assurance. S/he may delegate this to any group or individual, except for the project manager.

Illustration

Project: Small, simple, local

Jackie, the CEO of a small, privately-held business, appointed herself as executive for a small project. Even though the project was small in scale, she felt, as head of the company, she was in the best position to ensure that the project provided value for money. Additionally, Jackie planned on fulfilling the project assurance roles by mentoring the project manager and reviewing his/her work regularly.

Project: Large, complex, global

Jack, the CEO of a large multinational organization, took ownership of the project because of its importance to the future of the organization and his personal desire to ensure it contributed to the bottom line by expanding the business and profits. His strong belief in the project idea and the potential for the organization's future drove him to seek out and arrange funding from creative sources, such as partnership agreements, grants and the issuing of common stocks. With the aid of the finance director and legal counsel performing business assurance at every step of the way, Jack was guaranteed a sound business investment in the project.

Senior user

Description:

The senior user(s) is responsible for specifying the needs of those who will use the project's products, for user liaison with the project management team, and for monitoring that the solution will meet those needs within the constraints of the business case in terms of quality, functionality and ease of use.

The role represents the interests of all those who will use the project's products (including operations and maintenance), those for whom the products will achieve an objective or those who will use the products to deliver benefits. The senior user role commits user resources and monitors products against requirements. The role may require more than one person to cover all the user interests. For the sake of effectiveness, the role should not be split between too many people.

What this means

Someone in management from the customer organization needs to represent the user interests throughout the project. The users will be those groups or individuals who will use or be impacted by the project's products. The senior user will ensure, from a management perspective, that the products are being created, tested and approved with the users in mind. Additionally, the products will need to be usable in order for them to be used. The only way to get benefits from a project is for the users to change their behavior (the outcome) by using the project's products (the outputs). The senior user will thus help specify and define the projects, and will be held accountable for their realization, even after the project concludes.

The senior user has responsibility for the function of user assurance. He/She/They may delegate this to any group or individual, except for the project manager.

Illustration

Project: Small, simple, local

Guillermo put his name into the pot to be the senior user for the new automated phone system project. He currently supervises the team of call centre staff who will be trialing the new system for the company. He has progressed his career through the ranks, so feels he is in an excellent position to understand the needs of his staff and what is in their best interests.

Project: Large, complex, global

Willamina runs the directorate that will be most impacted by the project. She has insisted, from the beginning, that she be on the project board in the role of senior user. She shares this role with the director of sales and the director of market research. Together, they represent the internal staff and end users worldwide. As directors in the organization, they recognize that they are too busy to fulfill their own project assurance, and have each delegated this responsibility to one or more middle managers within their directorates. Additionally, their project assurance delegates will also form a global user group to take in ideas and feedback about the project. This information will be collected and fed back to the three senior users to help them in their formal role representing the user community.

Senior supplier

Description:

The senior supplier represents the interests of those designing, developing, facilitating, procuring and implementing the project's products. This role is accountable for the quality of products delivered by the supplier(s) and is responsible for the technical integrity of the project. If necessary, more than one person may be required to represent the suppliers.

Depending on the particular customer/supplier environment, the customer may also wish to appoint an independent person or group to carry out assurance on the supplier's products (for example, if the relationship between the customer and supplier is a commercial one).

What this means

Someone in management from either the customer and/or an external supplier organization needs to represent the supplier interests throughout the project. The suppliers are those individuals or groups of specialist and technical workers who will supply the project's specialist products. Typically, under business as usual conditions, the senior supplier is the line manager above the suppliers. He/she/they will be held accountable for the quality of products supplied by the suppliers.

The senior supplier has responsibility for the function of supplier assurance. He/She/They may delegate this to any group or individual, except for the project manager.

Illustration

Project: Small, simple, local

Charles is the account manager at a small web design firm. He has two designers working on the front-end interface for the new website ordered by the client. He will represent the web design firm's interests during the two-month project.

Project: Large, complex, global

Chelsea is the top sales executive for IGM Financial Inc. As IGM is the major supplier for the client's new bespoke IGM-based international investment system, Chelsea is performing the senior supplier role. She will share this role with other major suppliers internal and external to the client organization. As the lead supplier, however, she will also chair a separate supplier group of all the suppliers. They will meet monthly to discuss technical aspects of the project, and Chelsea will ensure that they stay coordinated and efficient in their efforts.

Project manager

Description:

The project manager has the authority to run the project on a day-to-day basis on behalf of the project board within the constraints laid down by them.

The project manager's prime responsibility is to ensure that the project produces the required products within the specified tolerances of time, cost, quality, scope, risk and benefits. The project manager is also responsible for the project producing a result of achieving benefits defined in the business case.

What this means

The project manager reports to and takes direction from the project board. S/he has the day-to-day control over the project for a stage at a time. As long as s/he is inside – and predicted to remain inside – the stage-level tolerances, s/he has authority to make decisions about the stage. In order to maintain control over the stage without actually doing the work, the project manager must be good at people management, communications, negotiation and delegation.

Illustration

Project: Small, simple, local

Stephanie is a full-time project manager. She currently manages four small projects within her organization. Two of her projects are coming to a close soon, so she feels she can take on another one. This new one is also quite small and within her area of expertise, so she feels it will be a good fit and good timing.

Project: Large, complex, global

Steven is a full-time project manager dedicated to one project. He has two junior managers assisting him with his management responsibilities, as well as a project support team that is in charge of the project's administration duties. In order to stay on top of the project, Steven meets with his assistants and the rest of project support every morning for a brief 20-minute update meeting on Skype®. The only rule for the meeting is that there are no rules. Anything is allowed to be surfaced. However, agenda items requiring more time and attention will be dealt with offline, in separate meetings. Managing the project management this way, Steven feels that he is fostering an environment that is open and transparent, so issues will not be hidden.

Team manager

Description:
The team manager's prime responsibility is to ensure production of those products defined by the project manager to an appropriate quality, in a set timescale and at a cost acceptable to the project board. The team manager role reports to, and takes direction from, the project manager.

What this means

The individuals performing the team manager role within a project are the specialist and technical experts who either produce the project's specialist products or manage the team members who do. The team manager takes responsibility for the product creation as agreed in the work package. S/he ensures that the quality-checking activities planned for the products are carried out correctly, with the results updated in the quality register. While creating the products, the team manager sends regular progress information to the project manager via checkpoint reports. All finished work is handed back to the project manager in the fashion and manner agreed in the work package.

Illustration

Project: Small, simple, local

Pollyanna has recently earned her PhD degree in her highly specialized field. Her extensive knowledge in this field positions her well to be an ideal candidate for the team manager role. However, her work experience is quite limited. So, to start her off and introduce her to the culture, limitations and constraints of her new corporate environment, her new manager has asked her to use her skills on a small project. Her small team has been in the organization for some time, and will help her adjust to the move from academia to commerciality.

For every piece of specialist work that Pollyanna and her team attempts, Pollyanna first agrees the work and the constraints with a project manager. For up until she and her team have fully gelled as a team, Pollyanna has set an indiscriminate, temporary limit of three work packages that she and her team will take on at any point in time. As the work progresses in each of the work packages, Pollyanna checks in with her team members and then sends checkpoint reports via e-mails to the various project managers. Finally, as each piece of work is completed, she sends the completed products back to the project managers, usually by walking them over to their offices next door.

Project: Large, complex, global

Pier Paolo is one of 15 team managers working on the project during this stage. His role is to manage the co-located team in Portugal, Spain and southern France. He meets with his team members in person on a weekly basis, and gets feedback from them via e-mail on a daily basis. He regularly speaks with two other team managers who are working on related products in other regions. He provides weekly checkpoint reports via e-mail to the project manager, in which he gives updates about his progress according to his team plan. So far, he has only had to raise one issue about a small delay that took him out of his work package tolerances. The issue was resolved by the project manager, who gave him extra time tolerance to cover the delay.

Project assurance

Description:

Project assurance covers the primary stakeholder interests (business, user and supplier).

Project assurance has to be independent of the project manager; therefore the project board cannot delegate any of its assurance activities to the project manager.

What this means

Technically, project assurance is not a separate role, but a function or responsibility of the project board members. If the project board members find that they are too busy or do not have the required skills to fulfill this function, they are allowed to delegate it to an individual or group of individuals, as long as the person or group is independent of the project manager.

The purpose of the project assurance is to review, check and advise the project manager (along with project support and the team managers) in their performance of managing the project. Specialist products will be checked and reviewed by objective specialists in well-defined quality reviews. Management products need to be checked and reviewed by objective persons carrying out the project assurance function covering the business, user and supplier perspectives. Because this function exists as an integral part of the PRINCE2® framework, the project board can rest assured that any information they receive from the project manager has been reviewed or checked first by project assurance.

Illustration

Project: Small, simple, local

Marcia is the executive, senior user and senior supplier for the project. She has decided to perform all of her project assurance responsibilities. Over the next six weeks – the length of the project – it is not worth bringing in and paying for extra resources to perform these duties, which she truly believes she will have time to take on. It will be tight, of course, and require some overtime on her part, but for this short project, she feels this is the best solution.

Project: Large, complex, global

Marcus performs the user assurance activities for the senior user of the project. He reviews all the product descriptions, including the project product description from the users' perspectives. He checks that they accurately reflect the true purpose of the products and examines the quality criteria and tolerances to ensure they are within acceptable limits for the users. Marcus advises the project manager on who should be chosen as an appropriate reviewer to test the products when they are complete. He reports regularly to the senior users, assuring them that the project manager is doing quality work and focusing on creating usable products. Finally, Marcus also liaises with the two other individuals who are performing user assurance to take care that they do not step on each others' responsibilities, overload the project manager, or, worse yet, provide conflicting guidance to the project manager.

Manuela performs similar tasks on behalf of the executive of the project. Her focus, however, is to advise and review project work to ensure that the project remains focused on achieving its objectives and delivering products that will achieve the benefits. In order to do this, she assists the project manager in developing the business case and benefits review plan. Her typical duties involve verifying, checking and reviewing the financial aspects of the project, all the while focusing on the continued viability of the project.

Finally, Monte has been assigned to perform supplier assurance for the same project. His expertise in writing requirements comes in handy when he has to review product descriptions that detail quality criteria for each of the project's specialist products. His responsibilities center on advising and monitoring the management of the product creation from start to finish. He not only reviews how the products have been described in product descriptions, but also advises on the right method(s) to create the products. Additionally, he assesses whether the quality control methods will, in fact, correctly test that the products meet their quality criteria.

Change authority

Description:

The project board may delegate authority for approving responses to requests for change or off-specifications to a separate individual or group, called a change authority. The project manager could be assigned as the change authority for some aspects of the project (e.g. changing baselined work packages if it does not affect stage tolerances).

What this means

Technically, change authority is not a separate role, but a function or responsibility of the project board members. If the project board members find that they are too busy or not have the required technical skills to fulfill this function, they are allowed to delegate it to an individual or group of individuals, including the project manager.

The purpose of the change authority is to review and approve or reject all requests for change and off-specifications (missing or incomplete products). The change authority function can be split and divided among many individuals if the technical complexity of the project calls for it. If a change budget is created, the change authority may use this within their delegated limits for approving changes. Sometimes, the best person to review and approve or reject a change is the person who is currently working on the product being impacted: the team manager. If the project board feels that a certain team manager has the right skill sets, or they trust his/her judgment about changes, they can pass part or all of their change authority function to him/her.

Illustration

Project: Small, simple, local

Tony is the project manager, project support and team manager for his project. His boss (the executive) has delegated most of the change authority function to him, as well. He is authorized to make decisions about changes up to a £1000 limit at a time. His total change budget is

£15,000. Any change(s) requiring more than £1000 at a time, or causing the spend to exceed the total change budget of £15,000, will call for Tony to escalate the change to his boss.

Project: Large, complex, global

Tawnya sits on a design board within her organization. The design board contributes their extensive technical and specialist knowledge and expertise to the project as the change authority. Impact analyses of requests for change and off-specifications require in-depth investigations and comprehensive understandings of the intricacies of the organization's existing and future systems. Tawnya and the design board assist the project manager with these analytical examinations and propose options for dealing with the potentially complicated modifications. Then, as a group, they decide on the best approach.

Project support

Description:
The provision of any project support on a formal basis is optional. If it is not delegated to a separate person or function it will need to be undertaken by the project manager.
One support function that must be considered is that of configuration management. Depending on the project size and environment, there may be a need to formalize this and it may become a task with which the project manager cannot cope without support.

What this means

The larger and more complex a project is, the bigger the need for a separate person or people to fulfill the project support role. Project support aids with the project administration. He/She/They must have administrative skills, be organized, and pay attention to detail. Collecting information and keeping records up to date is a primary function, especially for configuration management over the project's management and specialist products.

Illustration

Project: Small, simple, local

Helena worked on the project team as project support for 10% of her time. This meant she spent, on average, four hours a week ensuring that records were up to date, filed in the right place and correctly labeled. Periodically, she attended project meetings. There, she took the minutes, but mostly, she filed documents, stored specialist products in a cupboard, and e-mailed reports to defined distribution lists.

Project: Large, complex, global

Ellen managed a support team of 20 staff members. Together, they supported two programs and five stand-alone projects. Their duties included configuration management, workshop facilitation, and mentoring of project managers – especially in planning tools and estimating methods. Their well-defined systems and expertise in organization kept the most up-to-date information flowing to the right people at the right times.

CHAPTER 15: MANAGEMENT PRODUCTS

> *Management products are not necessarily documents, they are information sets that are used by the PRINCE2® processes, so that certain roles can take action and/or make decisions.*

The following list of management products is in alphabetical order.

Benefits review plan

> ## PURPOSE:
>
> *A benefits review plan is used to define how and when a measurement of the achievement of the project's benefits, expected by the senior user, can be made.*

When is it created? When is it updated?

- Created during the Initiating a Project process
- Updated during the Managing a Stage Boundary and Closing a Project processes, or – when requested by the project board via ad hoc direction – using the project's formal change control procedures.

Illustration

Project: Small, simple, local

Based on the executive's request, Obe's benefits review plan was not a separate document, but rather an additional section in the business case, listing the proposed dates and measures for all the benefits justifying the project to be assessed.

Project: Large, complex, global

Onawara created an extensive benefits review plan, which explained how and when each of the project's benefits should be measured post-project. Her detailed instructions included resource requirements needed for the measurements and the desired skill sets to perform the reviews.

Business case

PURPOSE:

A business case is used to document the justification for the undertaking of a project, based on the estimated costs (of development, implementation and incremental ongoing operations and maintenance costs) against the anticipated benefits to be gained and offset by any associated risks.

When is it created? When is it updated?

- Created in outline form during the Starting up a Project process
- Created fully during the Initiating a Project process
- Updated during the Managing a Stage Boundary and Closing a Project processes, or – when requested by the project board via ad hoc direction – using the project's formal change control procedures.

Illustration

Project: Small, simple, local

Sheila's outline business case was a section of her project brief, which was captured on the back of a serviette. Her full business case was more formal than that. It was captured in an e-mail to her boss, along with the other considerations for the project initiation documentation.

Project: Large, complex, global

Shawn's business case covered 10 sides of A4 paper, and fully documented and described the benefits, drawbacks, timescales, costs and major risks. It was distributed to the 17 senior managers within the organization for review, and only approved after external scrutiny from a financial advisor.

Checkpoint report

PURPOSE:

A checkpoint report is used to report, at a frequency defined in the work package, the status of the work package.

When is it created? When is it updated?

- Created during the Managing Product Delivery process
- Not updated – new reports are created to provide updated progress information.

Illustration

Project: Small, simple, local

Scarlett, the team manager, leaned over her desk and told Johan, the project manager, that she was almost finished with one thing and about to start on another. Johan noted it in his notebook (the daily log).

Project: Large, complex, global

Seamus personally interviewed every member of his team to find out the statuses of their products, and what issues, risks and concerns they had. He marked their progress on his team plan, wrote up a report using the approved checkpoint report template, and sent it to the project manager, copying in project support and project assurance.

Communication management strategy

PURPOSE:

A communication management strategy contains a description of the means and frequency of communication to parties both internal and external to the project. It facilitates engagement with stakeholders through the establishment of a controlled and bidirectional flow of information.

When is it created? When is it updated?

- Created during the Initiating a Project process
- If required, updated during the Managing a Stage Boundary process.

Illustration

Project: Small, simple, local

Ethan referenced the corporate communication management strategy and noted that all project team communication between himself and the executive would most likely be verbal, and backed up with e-mails stored in his e-mail system.

Project: Large, complex, global

Abby referenced the corporate communication strategy and documented the variances her project would be making in order to accommodate the 15 external suppliers, the tools they would be using, and the intricate feedback loop mechanism designed especially for this project. All stakeholders were identified and analyzed by local or regional teams to provide the most insight and cultural nuances possible.

Configuration item record

PURPOSE:

To provide a record of such information as the history, status, version and variant of each configuration item, and any details of important relationships between them. The set of configuration item records for a project is often referred to as a configuration library.

When is it created? When is it updated?

- Created as soon as the need for a product has been identified, using the same unique identifier cited on the product description for the product
- Updated during the Controlling a Stage, Managing Product Delivery, Managing a Stage Boundary and Closing a Project processes.

Illustration

Project: Small, simple, local

Dalia kept a Microsoft® Excel® spreadsheet that tracked the five criteria for the seven main products of her project.

She tracked:

1. Unique item identifiers
2. Version numbers
3. Statuses
4. Relationships with each other
5. Any issue numbers that caused changes to the products.

Dalia was the project manager, team manager and the project support for this project. For this reason, she didn't need to track anything else; as she would be the one to own the products, they'd be located in her office and worked on only during the delivery stage of the project.

Project: Large, complex, global

Leonard used a database to keep track of 50 separate criteria for his project's products. Access to the database was limited to authorized configuration librarians in order to ensure tight control over the information. Each member of the configuration librarian team was responsible for updating the criteria for up to five items at a time. The number of changes to a single item per day could run in the hundreds.

Configuration management strategy

PURPOSE:

A configuration management strategy is used to identify how and by whom, the project's products will be controlled and protected.

It answers the questions:

- *How and where the project's products will be stored*
- *What storage and retrieval security will be put in place*
- *How the products and the various versions and variants of these will be identified*
- *How changes to products will be controlled*
- *Where responsibility for configuration management will lie.*

When is it created? When is it updated?

- Created during the Initiating a Project process
- If required, updated during the Managing a Stage Boundary process.

Illustration

Project: Small, simple, local

Lolita referenced her corporate configuration management strategy and noted that this project would use local Microsoft® Excel® spreadsheets to capture the project's configuration item records for the issue register. They would be held on the project manager's C: drive, with read-only access for everyone but the project manager.

Project: Large, complex, global

Damian managed of team of 20 staff to identify, track and protect the project's products. They used a massive database to track the different product variations and states with utmost attention to detail. Damian's project involved minute chemical combinations that could have had disastrous effects if even one item was mislabeled or misplaced. Access to Damian's project products required a "security 3 level" credential.

Daily log

PURPOSE:

A daily log is used to record informal issues, required actions or significant events not caught by other PRINCE2®️ registers or logs. It acts as the project diary for the project manager.

When is it created? When is it updated?

- Created during the Starting Up a Project process
- Updated during the Initiating a Project, Controlling a Stage, Managing a Stage Boundary and Closing a Project processes by the project manager
- If the team manager also uses a daily log, then it is created and updated during the Managing Product Delivery process.

Illustration

Project: Small, simple, local

Fabienne – fulfilling the roles of project manager, team manager and project support – used her daily log as her combined daily log, lessons log, issue register, risk register and quality register throughout the project.

Project: Large, complex, global

Jacob used a 200-page loose-leaf binder as his daily log. He captured everything in it – from conversations to ideas, thoughts, concerns and observations about the project. He reviewed his daily log every two hours to ensure that he transferred his notes to the appropriate management product. Although he liked to use paper, he requested that his team managers use personal digital assistance (PDAs) that would link into his computer, so he could review their notes and see if he needed to add them to any formal project documentation.

End project report

PURPOSE:

An end project report is used during project closure to review how the project performed against the version of the project initiation documentation used to authorize it. It also allows the:

- *Passing on of any lessons that can be usefully applied to other projects*
- *Passing on of details of unfinished work, ongoing risks or potential product modifications to the group charged with future support of the project's products in their operational life.*

When is it created? When is it updated?

- Created during the Closing a Project process – either as part of a planned or premature closure
- Not updated.

Illustration

Project: Small, simple, local

Paco reviewed the project initiation documentation – which had been created six weeks earlier – and compared the final product with it. There were some minor differences, which he explained by reviewing the risk and issue registers. He summed up his findings in an e-mail to the project executive (the end project report).

Project: Large, complex, global

Yancey and four members of her team spent five full days preparing to write the end project report. They reviewed the original PID – which had been created by Yancy's predecessor six years ago – and then combed through the various revised versions updated throughout the project. After a thorough appraisal, Yancey was able to give a complete assessment of the project efforts (the end project report).

End-stage report

PURPOSE:

An end-stage report is used to give a summary of progress to date, the overall situation, and sufficient information to ask for a project board decision on what to do next with the project.

When is it created? When is it updated?

* Created during the Managing a Stage Boundary process
* Not updated: new reports are issued at the end of every delivery stage, except for the final one; an end project report is issued at the end of the final stage.

Illustration

Project: Small, simple, local

Balthasar recapped his initiation stage experience as his one and only end-stage report, and sent it in an e-mail to the executive. He did not need to write another one for his project, as there was only one delivery stage. At the end of that stage, he would write the end project report.

Project: Large, complex, global

Warren reviewed his previous highlight reports from this stage and cut and pasted any relevant information into his end-stage report. He added the final touches about the last piece of work and his assessment of how the stage went. He pulled a stage-level status accounting report to prove all the products from this stage had, in fact, been completed, tested and approved. He then sent this information to project assurance to review, before sending it on to the project board for approval.

Exception report

PURPOSE:

An exception report is produced when a stage plan or project plan is forecast to exceed tolerance levels set. It is prepared by the project manager in order to inform the project board of the situation, and to offer options and recommendations for the way to proceed.

When is it created? When is it updated?

- Created during the Controlling a Stage process, when the stage-level tolerances are forecast to be exceeded
- Updated as decisions and resolutions are confirmed and implemented regarding the exception.

Illustration

Project: Small, simple, local

Nadia picked up the phone and dialed the number for her boss (who was also the project's executive). She gave a quick rundown of the exception situation and a brief recap of the ideas she had to deal with it. She also confirmed that she would now sit down and send this information to her again via e-mail, but needed to give her boss the immediate heads-up first.

Project: Large, complex, global

Masood had been reviewing the impact of the issue with three members of project assurance to get the best estimates of how big the problem was. The issue had been captured by one of his team managers, who entered it in a formal issue report. It was now evident that Masood would have to escalate this issue via an exception report. He telephoned the executive to give him an early verbal warning, and then created the formal exception report. He then distributed it to the entire project board, as well as to other members from corporate and program management who, as indicated in the communication strategy, were needing to be kept in the loop of exception situations.

Highlight report

PURPOSE:

A highlight report is used to provide the project board (and possibly other stakeholders) with a summary of the stage status at intervals defined by them. The project board uses the report to monitor stage and project progress. The project manager also uses it to advise the project board of any potential problems or areas where the project board could help.

When is it created? When is it updated?

- Created during the Controlling a Stage process and at the frequency defined by the project board
- Not updated – new reports are created to provide updated progress information.

Illustration

Project: Small, simple, local

Janice, the project manager, had her weekly one-on-one manager meeting with her boss, the executive. She included progress information (a highlight report) about the three projects she was managing.

Project: Large, complex, global

With the aid of her project support team, Zelda reviewed and assessed all the checkpoint reports from the team managers to glean the highlights to report to the project board. They looked through the issue, risk and quality registers to find any new items worth including in the reporting. They double-checked the product checklist to ensure all the products listed for this period had actually been completed. The highlight report was then assembled, reviewed by project assurance for accuracy, and then sent on to the project board and other interested stakeholders identified on the communication management strategy.

Issue register

PURPOSE:

The purpose of the issue register is to capture and maintain information on all of the issues that are being formally managed. The issue register should be monitored by the project manager on a regular basis.

When is it created? When is it updated?

- Created during the Initiating a Project process; any issues identified earlier will be transferred from the daily log to the issue register
- Updated during the Initiating a Project, Controlling a Stage, Managing a Stage Boundary and Closing a Project processes.

Illustration

Project: Small, simple, local

Nora – fulfilling the roles of project manager, team manager and project support – used her daily log as her issue register throughout the project.

Project: Large, complex, global

Philip created a bespoke web-enabled issue register database that could be accessed by all team members around the world. Entry into the register was no longer restricted by time zones. Any team member anywhere in the world could make an entry. Project support reviewed the database four times a day and called the author(s) if there were any questions. Philip assessed the new entries every day for at least one hour, taking corrective action where he had the authority to do so, or escalating them (in an exception report) where he did not.

Issue report

PURPOSE:

An issue report is a report containing the description, impact assessment and recommendations for a request for change, off-specification or problem/concern. It is only created for those issues that need to be handled formally.

When is it created? When is it updated?

- Created at any time from the initiation stage onwards, where an issue has been identified that needs to be formally managed. If authority has been delegated to the team manager to use the issue report, then s/he would create one during the Managing Product Delivery process. Otherwise, the project manager will create them during the Initiating a Project and Controlling a Stage processes.
- Updated as decisions and resolutions are confirmed and implemented regarding the issue during the Initiating a Project, Controlling a Stage, Managing a Stage Boundary and Closing a Project processes.

Illustration

Project: Small, simple, local

Wendy used e-mail to capture formal issues that she wanted to get to the attention of the project board (her boss). The threaded e-mail discussions also captured the final decisions made. Wendy was also able to use the dates and times on the e-mails to organize and arrange the issues in a folder on her desktop.

Project: Large, complex, global

Francis used the program's official issue report template to capture issues. When authorizing work packages to his team managers, he included the template for them to use as well. Project support used a document management system to track and store all the issue reports from the project. Project assurance checked and reviewed the reports to make sure that all the team members were using the correct and latest version of the template.

Lessons log

> ### PURPOSE:
>
> *The lessons log is a project repository for lessons that apply to this project or future projects. Some lessons may originate from other projects and should be captured on the lessons log for input to the project's strategies and plans. Some lessons may originate from within the project – where new experience (both good and bad) can be passed to others via a lessons report.*

When is it created? When is it updated?

* Created during the Starting Up a Project process
* Updated whenever a lesson is learned, or, at the very least, at the end of each stage during the Managing a Stage Boundary and Closing a Project processes.

Illustration

Project: Small, simple, local

Farrah – fulfilling the roles of project manager, team manager and project support – used her daily log to capture lessons throughout the project.

Project: Large, complex, global

Michael had monthly meetings with his team managers and members of project assurance to ensure they were capturing lessons as they progressed through the project. Many of the lessons were learned through risks and issues experienced on the project and reflections on how these could have been predicted more accurately or avoided through better planning. The lessons log was filed with the official project documentation administered by project support. Any new lessons identified in their review meetings were added to the log by project support, cross-referencing the risk register or issue register where appropriate.

Lessons report

PURPOSE:

The lessons report is used to pass on any lessons that can be usefully applied to other projects.

The purpose of the report is to provoke action, so that the positive lessons become embedded in the organization's way of working, and that the organization is able to avoid any negative lessons on future projects.

When is it created? When is it updated?

- Created during the Managing a Stage Boundary and/or Closing a Project processes
- Not updated – new reports may be issued when major or important lessons need to be distributed and shared with the rest of the organization.

Illustration

Project: Small, simple, local

Kaelem reserved an agenda item in the final project meeting to discuss the ups and downs of the project experience with his team. He captured the sentiments in the meeting minutes (the lessons report) and distributed these to the executive and other project managers in his department.

Project: Large, complex, global

Annie and her team wrote a comprehensive lessons report, which they shared with the project board and key stakeholders identified on the communication management strategy. The report was translated into six different languages and revised to meet the needs of local and regional cultures and customs, so that it could be shared around the entire organization. Another modified version was distributed to key suppliers who had additional, ongoing business relationships with the organization.

Plan

PURPOSE:

A plan provides a statement of how and when objectives are to be achieved, by showing the major products, activities and resources required for the scope of the plan. In PRINCE2®, there are three levels of plan: project, stage and team. Team plans are optional.

A plan should cover not just the activities to create products but also the activities to manage product creation – including activities for assurance, quality management, risk management, configuration management, communication and any other project controls required.

When is it created? When is it updated?

- Project plan
  - Created during the Initiating a Project process
  - Updated during the Managing a Stage Boundary and Closing a Project processes

- Stage plan or exception plan
  - Created during the Starting Up a Project and Managing a Stage Boundary processes
  - Updated during the Controlling a Stage and Closing a Project processes
- Team plan
  - If created, created during the Managing Product Delivery process
  - If created, updated during the Managing Product Delivery process.

Illustration

Project: Small, simple, local

For his one delivery stage project, Iago's project plan was also his stage plan. No team plans were required, as he was not only the project manager, but also the team manager.

Project: Large, complex, global

Gabriella's project plan and stage plans comprised of one version created using specialized planning software, a presentation version in Microsoft® PowerPoint®, and a product checklist version in Microsoft® Word®. In order to keep consistent records on progress, she required her team managers to use the same specialized planning software, but left it up to each team manager to determine if they required a presentational version and/or product checklist.

Product description

PURPOSE:

A product description is used to:

- *Understand the detailed nature, purpose, function and appearance of the product*
- *Define who will use the product*
- *Identify the sources of information or supply for the product*
- *Identify the level of quality required of the product*
- *Enable identification of activities to produce, review and approve the product*
- *Define the people or skills required to produce, review and approve the product.*

When is it created? When is it updated?

- Created as soon as the need for a product has been identified. High-level products are identified in the project plan during the Initiating a Project process. Lower-level products are identified in the stage plan made during the Managing a Stage Boundary process. Even smaller component products may require product descriptions for the team plan, which is created during the Managing Product Delivery process.
- Not updated – approved product descriptions are subject to the project's formal change control procedures.

Illustration

Project: Small, simple, local

Mackenzie – fulfilling the roles of project manager, team manager and project support – used her daily log to capture the requirements of the three main products she was required to create for her project.

Project: Large, complex, global

Lindsey used a bespoke requirements-capturing software package to define and analyze her project's products. The system was able to translate her product descriptions into up to 70 different languages and regional dialects.

Product status account

> ### PURPOSE:
>
> *The product status account provides information about the state of products within defined limits. The limits can vary. For example, the report could cover the entire project, a particular stage, a particular area of the project, or the history of a specific product. It is particularly useful if the project manager wishes to confirm the version number of products.*

When is it created? When is it updated?

- Created at any time after configuration item records have been created. The status account report will reflect all the statuses of the products defined for the report: i.e. Managing a Stage Boundary and Closing a Project.

- Not updated – later versions of the report may be pulled at later times.

Illustration

Project: Small, simple, local

Lakeisha was able to print her Microsoft® Excel® spreadsheet of her configuration item records at any point in time. This printed version acted as her product status account report.

Project: Large, complex, global

Horace required specialized reporting software to define and create his product status account reports. The software helped Horace set the reporting constraints from dropdown menus – such as the product's type, language, country of origin, status, state, variation, version, stage, owner, etc. It also allowed him to filter the report by date ranges.

Project brief

PURPOSE:

A project brief is used to provide a full and firm foundation for the initiation of the project and is created in the Starting up a Project process.

When is it created? When is it updated?

- Created during the Starting Up a Project process
- Not updated – information from the project brief may be used in the project initiation documentation, but the project brief does not, as a whole, get updated or included in that documentation.

Illustration

Project: Small, simple, local

Shelley's project brief was never actually written down. It was the result of her discussions with her manager, the project board executive.

Project: Large, complex, global

Ladarius's project brief was presented to him by the program manager. It stipulated the program's aims and how this project fitted in with them. It provided a wealth of information about how the project was expected to run and the project constraints and tolerances being allocated to it.

Project initiation documentation

PURPOSE:

The purpose of the project initiation documentation is to define the project, in order to form the basis for its management and an assessment of its overall success. The project initiation documentation gives the direction and scope of the project and (along with the stage plan) forms the "contract" between the project manager and the project board.

When is it created? When is it updated?

- Assembled during the Initiating a Project process. Information inside the PID is created throughout the Starting up a Project and Initiating a Project processes.
- If required, updated during the Managing a Stage Boundary process, or when requested by the project board via ad hoc direction using the project's formal change control procedures.

Illustration

Project: Small, simple, local

Serena held a formal one-day meeting with her manager (the project board executive) with a detailed agenda. The agenda covered all the points required for the project initiation documentation. All the requisite decisions were made and captured in the meeting. Serena used the meeting minutes as the documented PID, and had her boss formally approve it via e-mail confirmation.

Project: Large, complex, global

Vanessa worked with six members of her team over a period of three and a half months to produce the project's PID. They had countless consultations with project assurance, the project board members themselves and external experts while creating the right level of documentation to help manage and control the massive change effort successfully.

Project product description

PURPOSE:

The project product description is a special form of product description that defines what the project must deliver in order to gain acceptance. It is used to:

- *Gain agreement from the user on the project's scope and requirements*
- *Define the customer's quality expectations*
- *Define the acceptance criteria, method and responsibilities for the project.*

When is it created? When is it updated?

- Created as part of the project brief during the Starting up a Project process
- Created in full during the Initiating a Project process
- If required, updated during the Managing a Stage Boundary or – when requested by the project board via ad hoc direction – using the project's formal change control procedures.

Illustration

Project: Small, simple, local

Amanda – fulfilling the roles of project manager, team manager and project support – kept a picture of the final product on the wall of her office. She kept this in plain view, so that she would always focus on delivering exactly that.

Project: Large, complex, global

Marjorie's project product description evolved over several major scoping exercises with the user groups, supplier groups, project board members and legal representation from several countries. After negotiations about what was desired, what was possible, and what was legal and achievable, a working project product description was finally agreed. The final version demonstrated several key compromises on how it would be ultimately accepted by the senior users at the end of the project.

Quality management strategy

PURPOSE:

A quality management strategy is used to define the quality techniques and standards to be applied, and the various responsibilities for achieving the required quality levels, during the project.

When is it created? When is it updated?

• Created during the Initiating a Project process
• If required, updated during the Managing a Stage Boundary process.

Illustration

Project: Small, simple, local

Taylor referenced her corporate quality management system and noted that her colleague, Bill, would quality review all seven of the project's products both halfway through their completion and when they were completed.

Project: Large, complex, global

Brianna had to work with her key suppliers to complete the project's quality management strategy. Although she could reference a lot of the information from her company's quality management system, the project was reliant on the suppliers providing quality work to agreed quality standards – especially internationally recognized standards. Because of this, appropriate references were required from the supplier organization's quality management systems. Where there were overlaps or contradictions, the project board was called in to resolve the problems and to solidify their position.

Quality register

PURPOSE:

A quality register is used to summarize all quality management activities that are planned or have taken place, and provides information for the end-stage reports and end project report. Its purpose is to:

- *Issue a unique reference for each quality activity*
- *Act as a pointer to the quality records for a product*
- *Act as a summary of the number and type of quality activities undertaken.*

When is it created? When is it updated?

- Created during the Initiating a Project process, when the quality management strategy is defined; initial version will be blank
- Updated during the Controlling a Stage, Managing Product Delivery, Managing a Stage Boundary and Closing a Project processes.

Illustration

Project: Small, simple, local

Quentin – fulfilling the roles of project manager, team manager and project support – used his daily log as his quality register throughout the project.

Project: Large, complex, global

Narinda had a bespoke database created for her project. Project support staff members were the only ones with editor access to the database. They entered in the timings of planned quality activities from the project manager's stage plans. As products were completed and tested, team managers would call into project support to inform them of the quality check results. Project support would then update the database with this new information. This system of strict control and access to the quality register ensured that no fraudulent or dishonest changes could be made to quality check results. Project assurance performed ad hoc reviews and audits of the process to ensure it worked correctly.

Risk management strategy

> ### PURPOSE:
>
> *A risk management strategy describes the specific risk management techniques and standards to be applied and the responsibilities for achieving an effective risk management procedure.*

When is it created? When is it updated?

- Created during the Initiating a Project process
- If required, updated during the Managing a Stage Boundary process.

Illustration

Project: *Small, simple, local*

Carla referenced her corporate risk management system and noted that, even though all her risks could be captured and assessed in her daily log, risk owners would need to be – at least – in a managerial level within the organization.

Project: *Large, complex, global*

Kimberly referenced her organization's comprehensive risk management strategy. Over several years, the organization had developed a highly tuned risk strategy based on their experiences in international and highly competitive industries. Because of this investment in defining this strategy, the project had little option but to comply with it fully. Specific information about how Kimberly's project team would divide and allocate risk management activities was all that could be adjusted for this effort. All other areas required strict adherence – for example, to risk categories, scales for impact and probability, reporting requirements, etc.

Risk register

PURPOSE:

A risk register provides a record of identified risks relating to the project, including their status and history. It is used to capture and maintain information on all the identified threats and opportunities relating the project.

When is it created? When is it updated?

- Created during the Initiating a Project process. Any risks identified earlier will be transferred from the daily log to the risk register.
- Updated during the Initiating a Project, Controlling a Stage, Managing a Stage Boundary and Closing a Project processes.

Illustration

Project: Small, simple, local

Tomasina – fulfilling the roles of project manager, team manager and project support – used her daily log as her risk register throughout the project.

Project: Large, complex, global

Martina's corporate risk management system served as the project's risk register. It had the functionality to assess the net present values (NPV) of risks and provide a realistic risk profile for the project. The system had been used by all the projects within the organization and was established as being foolproof.

Work package

PURPOSE:

A work package is a set of information about one or more required products collated by the project manager to pass responsibility for work or delivery formally to a team manager or team member.

When is it created? When is it updated?

- Created during the Controlling a Stage process by the project manager
- Possibly updated in the negotiations between the project manager and team manager in the authorization of and acceptance of the work package
- Possibly amended as a result of taking corrective action in reaction to an issue or risk.

Illustration

Project: Small, simple, local

Dale did not create any work packages. He was performing both the project manager and team manager roles and, therefore, didn't need the extra paperwork.

Project: Large, complex, global

Zita used the company's formal contract template to delegate work to team managers. The format ensured that the work was respected and given the attention it deserved, even from internal team managers. She required the team managers to sign and date the work packages when they accepted them. Copies of the work packages were also sent to the team managers' line managers, so that they fully understood the work their staff member was undertaking. For external team managers, Zita would issue formal feedback upon her work package status reviews. This, again, showed the suppliers how serious she was in managing and remaining in tight control over the project's work.

ITG RESOURCES

IT Governance Ltd. sources, creates and delivers products and services to meet the real-world, evolving IT governance needs of today's organizations, directors, managers and practitioners.

The ITG website (*www.itgovernance.co.uk*) is the international one-stop-shop for corporate and IT governance information, advice, guidance, books, tools, training and consultancy.

http://www.itgovernance.co.uk/project_governance.aspx is the page on our website for resources relevant to this book.

Other Websites

Books and tools published by IT Governance Publishing (ITGP) are available from all business booksellers and are also immediately available from the following websites:

www.itgovernance.co.uk/catalog/355 provides information and online purchasing facilities for every currently available book published by ITGP.

http://www.itgovernance.eu is our euro-denominated website which ships from Benelux and has a growing range of books in European languages other than English.

www.itgovernanceusa.com is a US$-based website that delivers the full range of IT Governance products to North America, and ships from within the continental US.

www.itgovernanceasia.com provides a selected range of ITGP products specifically for customers in South Asia.

www.27001.com is the IT Governance Ltd. website that deals specifically with information security management, and ships from within the continental US.

Pocket Guides

For full details of the entire range of pocket guides, simply follow the links at *www.itgovernance.co.uk/publishing.aspx*.

Toolkits

ITG's unique range of toolkits includes the IT Governance Framework Toolkit, which contains all the tools and guidance that you will need in order to develop and implement an appropriate IT governance framework for your organization. Full details can be found at *www.itgovernance.co.uk/ products/519*.

For a free paper on how to use the proprietary Calder-Moir IT Governance Framework, and for a free trial version of the toolkit, see *www.itgovernance.co.uk/calder_moir.aspx*.

There is also a wide range of toolkits to simplify implementation of management systems, such as an ISO/IEC 27001 ISMS or a BS25999 BCMS, and these can all be viewed and purchased online at: *http://www.itgovernance.co.uk/catalog/1*.

Best Practice Reports

ITG's range of Best Practice Reports is now at *www.itgovernance.co.uk/best-practice-reports.aspx*. These offer you essential, pertinent, expertly researched information on a number of key issues including Web 2.0 and Green IT.

ITG Resources

Training and Consultancy

IT Governance also offers training and consultancy services across the entire spectrum of disciplines in the information governance arena. Details of training courses can be accessed at _www.itgovernance.co.uk/training.aspx_ and descriptions of our consultancy services can be found at _http://www.itgovernance.co.uk/consulting.aspx_. Why not contact us to see how we could help you and your organization?

Newsletter

IT governance is one of the hottest topics in business today, not least because it is also the fastest moving, so what better way to keep up than by subscribing to ITG's free monthly newsletter _Sentinel_? It provides monthly updates and resources across the whole spectrum of IT governance subject matter, including risk management, information security, ITIL and IT service management, project governance, compliance and so much more. Subscribe for your free copy at: _www.itgovernance.co.uk/newsletter.aspx_.

Milton Keynes UK
Ingram Content Group UK Ltd.
UKHW021323050824
1157UKWH00069B/1089